The How-To Book

CANNING
FREEZING
DRYING

Written and compiled by
Anne Borella
Food Consultant

Barbara Bloch, Editor

APPRECIATION

Our sincere thanks go to the following for their helpful criticisms, comments, suggestions, and contributions.

Celia L. Fergusson, B.H.S., M.Sc., P.Dt. and Edmund S. Idziak, B.Sc. (Agr.), M.Sc., D.Sc., School of Food and Consumer Sciences, Macdonald Campus of McGill University; Agriculture Canada, Food Advisory Services; Consumer and Food Economics Institute, Agricultural Research Services, United States Department of Agriculture; GSW-Mirro, Housewares Division; Bernardin of Canada Ltd.; Sifto Salt Division, Domtar Chemicals, Ltd.; Hyla O'Connor.

Design by Gene Siegel
Illustrations by Axel Anderson & Richard Rosenblum

Original title: The Home Canning Handbook

ISBN: 0-87502-051-8
Copyright © 1974, 1976 by Dominion Glass Company Limited
All rights reserved.
Published by The Benjamin Company, Inc.
    485 Madison Avenue, New York, N.Y. 10022
Special edition for Leisure Technology, Inc.,
    Minneapolis, Minnesota
First Printing, revised edition: December 1976
Printed in the U.S.A.

CONTENTS

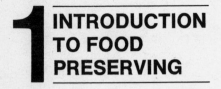

1 INTRODUCTION TO FOOD PRESERVING

This book is designed for the homemaker who is experienced in the art of food preservation, as well as those who may never have done any preserving before. It will point out the agents that cause spoilage in preserved food, describe the necessary equipment piece by piece, detail the different methods used for preserving, define terminology thoroughly and explain why procedures and instructions must be followed to the letter. We want you to know what you should do and why you are supposed to do it. Please read all the instructions carefully—once, or even twice. Always plan ahead and organize yourself before you begin cooking. This will help you work efficiently and streamline the process of preserving food. It will also make home-preserving simpler than you may have imagined and a great deal of fun.

As the cost of food continues to rise, more and more people are turning their backyards into vegetable gardens and watching their vegetables grow with a mixture of interest, pride and excitement. Even children find it exciting to see how cucumbers and squash grow and to discover how the runner bean got its name.

Today, keeping up with the Joneses means having the lowest monthly food bills on the block, as proof of the family's ingenuity and know-how in choosing and preparing food. As harvest time approaches, the prudent family gets together and works as a team to preserve the excess of each crop of fruit and vegetables in jars to be used during the winter.

Even if you don't have a garden, the abundance of local fresh fruit and vegetables on the market, or in open-air country stalls, should lure you into taking advantage of low cost, in-season produce. By putting up a selection of vegetables and fruit you can add interest and variety to meals during the winter months ahead, and at the same time save a substantial amount of money.

Whether you are planning to preserve for economy or fun, you'll find it rewarding and satisfying to see your pantry shelves stocked with an array of jars filled with the goodness of summer fruit and vegetables. You may even discover an unexpected dividend when your children develop a new interest in food they used to resist. If they have watched food grow and helped to preserve it, they may surprise you and eat it with pride—in spite of the fact that it is nutritious!

ANNUAL PRESERVING PLAN

You may decide to preserve only the excess of your garden crop. However, if you want to take advantage of the low prices of in-season produce, you can chart your family's food requirements for the months when certain food is out of season or is too expensive to include in meal planning. This will allow you to determine how much of each fruit or vegetable you should preserve.

Government-published nutrition guides tell us we should have two servings of fruit and vegetables everyday, one of which should be citrus fruit or tomatoes rich in vitamin C to insure a daily supply of this vitamin which the body does not store. The following food guide will help you meet the daily vitamin and mineral needs necessary for good health.

GUIDE TO FOOD PLANNING

Product	Vita-mins*	Number of Servings	Size of Servings	Amount per Person	For Family of Five
Citrus Fruit	C + +	3 per wk. 30 wks.	1 cup	22 qts.	110 qts.
Tomatoes & Tomato Juice	A & C+ A & C	4 per wk. 40 wks.	1 cup	40 qts.	200 qts.
Apples	C	2 per wk. 15 wks.	½ cup	4 qts.	20 qts.
Berries		2 in 3 wks. 40 wks.	½ cup	3½ qts.	17 qts.
Cherries	A & C	2 in 3 wks. 40 wks.	½ cup	3½ qts.	17 qts.
Fruit Juices		2 per wk. 30 wks.	1 cup	15 qts.	75 qts.
Peaches	A & C	2 per wk. 40 wks.	½ cup	10 qts.	50 qts.
Pears		1 in 2 wks. 32 wks.	½ cup	2 qts.	10 qts.
Plums		1 in 2 wks. 40 wks.	½ cup	2½ qts.	12 qts.
Asparagus	A & C	1 in 2 wks. 30 wks.	½ cup	2 qts.	10 qts.
Beans, Green	A & C	2 per wk. 36 wks.	½ cup	9 qts.	45 qts.
Beans, Lima	A & B	1 in 2 wks. 36 wks.	½ cup	2¼ qts.	11 qts.
Beets	C	1 per wk. 30 wks.	½ cup	4 qts.	20 qts.
Carrots	A+	2 per wk. 12 wks.	½ cup	3 qts.	15 qts.
Corn, Yellow	A	1 per wk. 38 wks.	¼ cup	3 qts.	15 qts.
Greens	A+ +	2 per wk. 16 wks.	½ cup	4 qts.	20 qts.
Okra	A & C	Occasionally 36 wks.	½ cup	2 pts.	10 pts.
Peas	A & C	1 per wk. 38 wks.	¼ cup	5 pts.	25 pts.
Sauerkraut		1 in 2 wks. 40 wks.	½ cup	2½ qts.	13 qts.
Succotash	A & B	Occasionally 36 wks.	½ cup	1 qt.	5 qts.
Jellies		2 per wk. 52 wks.	2 tsp.	13½ pts.	67½ pts.
Preserves		2 per wk. 52 wks.	2 tsp.	13½ pts.	67½ pts.
Pickles		1 per wk.			30 pts.

*If the vitamin is listed, it is present in an amount that is important to nutrition. If the food is a good source, it is indicated by one plus sign. If it occurs in a considerable quantity, two plus signs are used.

PRESERVING

Food spoils due to the action of microorganisms, which are all around us, and of enzymes, a complex group of chemicals found naturally in food. Although these agents are invisible to the eye, the home-preserver must be aware of their presence and the conditions that encourage their survival and reproduction, so she can select the correct technique to control, inactivate or destroy them.

Preserving is the application of scientifically tested procedures which allow food to be stored safely in the best condition over an extended period of time without the growth or action of food spoilage agents.

The food preservation methods covered in this book include heating, freezing, and drying. Properly done, each of these will destroy or inactivate food spoilage agents. Heated sterile food must be packed in hermetically-sealed (airtight) jars to prevent recontamination and insure safe consumption. Frozen food must be kept frozen until ready to use, then defrosted under sanitary conditions. Dried food may be stored under normal conditions. Once you have familiarized yourself with the techniques involved, you will have a wonderful selection of delicious recipes to choose from.

SPOILAGE AGENTS
Enzymes

Enzymes are chemical substances found in all living things. They are capable of causing both desirable and undesirable changes in food, and are helpful in regulating the metabolism of animals, in ripening fruit and in tenderizing meat. If their activity in fruit and vegetables is not terminated at the proper degree of ripeness, the enzymes will continue to work until the food is no longer palatable. They are responsible for causing changes in colour, flavour and texture of food. Enzymes are inactivated or destroyed by heat. However, if food is heated too slowly during preserving, enzymes may act before being inactivated. For example, in jars of light-coloured fruit, such as peaches, pears and apples, when time between packing the jars and processing is delayed, or when the water-bath processor takes too long to reach the boiling point, the enzyme has an opportunity to act. The result is unattractive fruit which can only be served when the electricity fails.

Microorganisms

Since microorganisms are found everywhere, obviously they will be found in food. Yeasts, moulds and bacteria are the microorganisms that affect food. Like enzymes, certain organisms can cause desirable effects in food. However, most of them are responsible for undesirable effects which result in food spoilage. Some forms of food spoilage cause changes in appearance, smell, texture or taste; others are not easily apparent.

Salt, sugar and moisture affect and influence the growth of moulds, yeasts and bacteria. Without moisture these organisms cannot grow—they simply lie in a dormant state until favourable conditions reactivate them.

Moulds

Mould spoilage is easy to spot. You can see the fluffy growth that appears in a multitude of colours—white, grey, black, red, green, blue—depending upon the kind of mould. They produce spores which dry and float through the air, fall on food or other suitable organic material, and begin their growth cycle.

Moulds grow on a wide variety of food—acidic foods like oranges and lemons, neutral food like bread and meat, and sweet food such as jams and jellies. Although they prefer moist dark places and temperatures from 70° to 90°F, they can also grow at refrigerator temperatures. Moulds usually can be destroyed by brief boiling.

Some moulds produce harmful substances which if eaten can accumulate in the system and eventually cause illness. Therefore, jams, jellies, conserves, preserves, etc., that show any sign of mould should be discarded.

Yeasts

Yeasts require moisture, sugar and air for growth. They can convert sugar into carbon dioxide and alcohol. Some food, such as fruit juice, will ferment if left at room temperature for any length of time. The juice will smell

9

and taste of alcohol, and become carbonated (i.e., it will contain bubbles of carbon dioxide).

Boiling will destroy yeasts. However, one of the problems in food preservation is recontamination which takes place when preserved food is inadequately protected, as is often the case with jams and jellies.

False or wild yeasts, always present in the atmosphere, affect pickling brines used to make cucumber pickles and sauerkraut. They are visible as a dry film on the surface. These yeasts use up the organic acid formed during fermentation.

Bacteria

Bacteria are microscopic, single-celled organisms which can multiply rapidly under favourable conditions. As with moulds and yeasts, some bacteria are useful in food preservation. Others cause food spoilage and a few even produce lethal toxins. Bacteria are used to cure cheese, produce vinegar, and cause desired changes in milk to make yogurt, buttermilk and sour cream. Brined pickles are preserved by the action of bacteria which form lactic acid.

Bacteria are considered to be the most active of all microorganisms and are therefore the most difficult to control. They vary greatly in their requirements for moisture, temperature, acidity, food and oxygen. Bacterial spoilage of preserved food is not always evident by appearance, smell, texture or taste, so it is important that the home-preserver be aware of the different types of bacteria that may cause spoilage and affect the safe preservation of food. Understanding the characteristics of various bacteria will enable you to realize the importance of carefully following all the instructions in this book.

All bacteria require water for growth. However, water used to dissolve large quantities of sugar or salt is not usually available to bacteria. In fact, the presence of sugar and salt may even promote the extraction of water from the bacterial cell. Therefore, jams and jellies do not normally permit bacterial growth.

Most bacteria prefer an almost neutral medium, one

10

that is neither acid nor alkaline. Some prefer a slightly acid medium while others prefer an alkaline medium.

The many varieties of bacteria differ in regard to the temperature at which they grow. A few can grow at refrigerator temperatures but the majority prefer temperatures between 68° to 113°F. A group of bacteria known as thermophiles find 95° to 180°F the most favourable temperature for growth, and form spores which are very resistant to heat. If not destroyed, some of them produce "flat-sour" spoilage in preserved food, while others produce gas as they grow. Processed preserved food must be cooled promptly to avoid the growth of these thermophilic bacteria.

Some bacteria are extremely resistant to heat. When conditions are unfavourable for growth, they form spores which are not easily destroyed by heat. These spores lie dormant until favourable conditions return, at which time they germinate and begin to grow again. *Clostridium botulinum* is one such bacterium. Its spores are resistant to processing in boiling water (212°F) for several hours and therefore temperatures much above boiling are required to eliminate it. This is accomplished through the use of a pressure processor to insure destruction. If it is not destroyed by heating it will begin to grow again, and produce a toxin or poison which is difficult to detect in appearance, smell or taste, and which is lethal in very tiny amounts. *Clostridium botulinum* is most active in low-acid vegetables, meat, poultry and fish. Therefore, all these foods *must* be processed in a steam-pressure processor at 240°F (10 lbs. pressure at sea level) for a scientifically-determined length of time.

Low-acid food, carefully prepared and processed for the correct length of time, in efficient pressure equipment that has an accurate pressure gauge, will not cause *botulism* poisoning. However, should the organism not be destroyed and eventually grow and produce toxin, this lethal substance can be destroyed by boiling the food for 10 minutes. Therefore, it is recommended that all low-acid home-preserved food such as seafood, poultry, meat, and all vegetables, except tomatoes, be boiled for 10 minutes before tasting or serving. Although this precautionary measure can be taken as an extra safeguard, it should not be an excuse for ignoring the recommendations in this book, or for adopting poor preserving methods.

Bacteria differ in their requirements for oxygen. Aerobic bacteria require oxygen for growth. Anaerobic bacteria are more at home in an airless environment. *Clostridium botulinum* is an anaerobic bacterium. If its spores have not been completely destroyed by heat during processing, they begin to grow and produce poison inside the hermetically-sealed jar.

Bacterial growth is inhibited or prevented by concentrations of salt and sugar. These ingredients are used as an aid in preservation where their addition complements or enhances the food, as sugar enhances fruit and jam and salt enhances vegetables.

In an acid medium many bacteria, including the spore-forming variety, are unable to grow. The presence of the acid during processing also enables bacteria to be destroyed more easily. Bacteria rarely remain active in fruit where acid is naturally present, in food to which vinegar has been added, or in food such as brined pickles and sauerkraut where acid results from fermentation. Bacteria are more difficult to destroy in low-acid fruit, vegetables, meat, poultry and seafood, and therefore all these foods must be processed in a steam-pressure processor at 240°F for the correct length of time. Generally, lower temperatures and shorter processing times are needed to destroy bacteria, moulds and yeasts in food with high-acid content, as compared to low-acid food.

Before pressure equipment for food preservation was easily available to the homemaker, all processing had to be done at 212°F. This was risky, since there was a possibility in low-acid food that dangerous spores would survive the heat.

CHEMICAL PRESERVATIVES

Chemicals and canning compounds should not be used for home preserving. All that is needed to preserve fruit and vegetables safely are airtight containers and

12

proper processing. Sulphur compounds, boracic acid, salicylic acid and saccharine are not permitted in commercial canning because they may prove harmful.

ROGUES GALLERY OF FOOD SPOILAGE AGENTS

Agents	ENZYMES
Hangouts	Fruit and vegetables
Special attractions for	Fruit and vegetables in the presence of oxygen
Wanted for	Darkening fruit and vegetables
How to inactivate	Apply temperature of 140°F or higher

Agents	MOULDS
Hangouts	In the air
Special attractions for	Jams, jellies, fruit and vegetables
Wanted for	Forming hair-like growths on jams, jellies, preserves, overripe fruit and vegetables
How to inactivate	Apply temperature of 212°F (boiling)

Agents	YEASTS
Hangouts	In the air
Special attractions for	Juices, jams, jellies, preserves, pickling brines and unrefrigerated fruit
Wanted for	Causing fermentation; forming dry film on pickling brine
How to inactivate	Apply temperature of 212°F (boiling)

Agents	**VEGETATIVE BACTERIA**
Hangouts	In the air, on hands, in dust, dirt and on equipment
Special attractions for	Low-acid food, temperatures above normal refrigerator temperature (40°F) and below pasteurization temperature (140°F)
Wanted for	Causing food to become soft and slimy
How to inactivate	Apply temperature of 212°F (boiling)

Agents	**THERMOPHILIC BACTERIA**
Hangouts	In the air, on hands, in dust, dirt and on equipment
Special attractions for	Low-acid food at temperatures from 100°F to 180°F
Wanted for	Causing "flat-sour"
How to inactivate	Cool processed food efficiently, do not leave at temperatures from 100°F to 180°F for prolonged period.

Agents	**SPORE-FORMING BACTERIA**
Hangouts	In the air, on hands, in dust, dirt and on equipment
Special attractions for	Low-acid food, insufficiently processed airtight containers
Wanted for	Producing deadly toxin
How to inactivate	Apply temperature of 240°F for time stated in recipe

Agents	TOXINS
Hangouts	Product of spore-forming bacterium **Clostridium botulinum**
Special attractions for	Underprocessed low-acid food preserved in anaerobic containers
Wanted for	Fatal poisoning
How to inactivate	Destroy by boiling food for 10 minutes before serving

PLANNING AND ORGANIZING

Efficiency in preserving depends upon good organization and good planning. The following tips will help insure streamlined, successful preserving of fruit and vegetables.

Plan several weeks ahead of the expected harvest of fruit and vegetables. If necessary, ask the produce manager at your local store when he expects each vegetable and fruit to be at its peak and at its lowest price.

Estimate your family's food needs (using the Guide to Food Planning on page 7) so you can preserve a variety of food in the correct amounts.

Calculate the number and size of jars and extra fittings you will need. Preserving has become very popular recently, so buy early to be sure you will have the equipment you need.

Organize an adequate storage area. Jars of preserved food should be stored in a cool, dark, dry place. Avoid storage areas where there is a risk of freezing, which can cause some jars to break or can spoil the texture of some food. An area that is too warm can be detrimental to flavour, and light can cause changes in the colour of preserved food. Jars should be wrapped in paper or placed in boxes to keep out light. An added precaution might be to find a storage area that is inaccessible to small children, hungry husbands and household pets.

Check your equipment against the equipment list on pages 23-28. Plan to buy or borrow whatever is needed.

Have the manufacturer check the gauge of your steam-pressure processor for accuracy.

Familiarize yourself with the operation of your steam-pressure processor.

SELECTING FRUIT AND VEGETABLES

Fruit has the best flavour when mature and ripe. Vegetables are best when they are young and tender. Watch the grades of food carefully and plan to do your preserving when produce reaches its peak quality. Sort for ripeness and preserve ripe produce immediately. Spread underripe fruit and vegetables on a tray to finish ripening. Bruised or spotted fruit should not be used for preserving. If bruises are cut away, the good portion of the fruit may be used for jams or fruit juices.

PRESERVING HINTS

Remember, preserving should never be done in over-large quantities. Do only as much as you can handle conveniently at one time. Have everything ready before you begin so all your time can be devoted to the care necessary for successful processing.

Try to devote full time to the project and let some of your regular routine fade into the background while you are preserving. This is an excellent time to recruit other members of the family for help with routine household chores and it will make the process of preserving much easier and the results of your efforts more gratifying.

Don't attempt to do too much in one day. After your first effort you will have a better idea of the amount of work you can do without getting tired. Working when tired can cause errors and bring about carelessness that will result in unsuccessfully preserved food.

Organize your kitchen before you begin. Put everything superfluous, such as kitchen ornaments, mixers, canisters, the family cat, etc., out of the way. Arrange your work area so you can conserve energy by sitting down as much as possible while preparing fruit and vegetables.

Follow a reliable, up-to-date recipe to the letter. Read the recipe all the way through before you begin. You may find, especially in pickling, that a vegetable or fruit must be salted or brined for several hours before you can proceed with the recipe.

Do not guess. Measure or weigh your fruit and sugar accurately. If you are hungry and the fruit looks too good to resist, eat a piece of fruit *before* you measure!

Read the manufacturer's instructions for fitting and sealing jars. Do not assume that all home-preserving caps are alike and fitted in the same manner. Failure to follow the proper method exactly can be a cause of sealing failure.

Estimate the number of jars to be used in a day of preserving. Be sure that every jar and lid is washed thoroughly and rinsed, at least twice, in hot water. Turn the jars upside down on a clean towel to air-dry until ready to use. Use clean, hot, soapy water and clean dishcloths.

Cleanliness is the major point in the preparation of all food to be preserved. It is absolutely necessary that preserving be done under the strictest sanitary conditions. Clean all your equipment and your entire work area thoroughly.

People with cuts, sores or colds should not be permitted to assist in food preservation. Their presence can add to the danger of food contamination by bacteria from their infection, which can result in food poisoning. If you are not feeling well, put off preserving until another day.

VITAMIN RETENTION IN HOME-PRESERVED FOOD

More and more people are aware of the food they eat and the importance of good nutrition. Homemakers who invest time, money and effort in preserving food want to be certain that the process they use will preserve food safely and will protect its nutritional value. Generally, there is little difference between the vitamin content of home-preserved food and the vitamin content of fresh food carefully prepared and cooked for immediate use.

Vitamins are destroyed or lost for a variety of reasons. Some vitamins are water soluble while others are fat soluble; some are more stable in acid while others are more stable in an alkaline medium. Some are destroyed by oxygen; some are destroyed by heat.

Because many vitamins and minerals are water soluble, the liquid portion of preserved fruit and vegetables contains significant quantities of water soluble vitamins and minerals. When fruit is served the juice is eaten with the fruit and these vitamins and minerals are not lost. The vitamin and mineral rich liquid from preserved vegetables may be saved and used in soup, sauces, gravies, etc. This liquid can be frozen and used at a later date.

ESTIMATING QUANTITIES

Most recipes are specific, but some preserving recipes can present a problem. How is a cook to shop for six cups of apricot pulp or four cups of berry juice? Part of the difficulty in providing accurate equivalents is the problem of determining how many tomatoes equal six cups when diced, or how many pounds make one quart—it depends on the size of the tomatoes. The following table therefore is intended to provide a guide for the confused shopper rather than precise information.

Produce	Pounds (as picked) required to pack quart jar	Volume container	Average weight (pounds) of container	Equivalent measure (per pound)
Apples Applesauce	2½–3 2½–3½	box or carton	40–45	4 small or 3 medium apples; 3 cups sliced
Apricots	2½–3	lug	24–26	8–14 apricots; 2 cups halved
Berries	1½–3	flat (12 1-pint boxes)	11–12	1½–3¼ cups
Cherries	2–2½	Campbell lug Calex lug	15 18–20	3 cups unpitted; 2 cups pitted
Peaches	2–3	Western peach box lug wire-bound crate or carton	16–18 19–22 38	4 medium peaches; 1½ cups sliced
Pears	2–3	lug tight-filled carton box or carton	21–26 36 45–48	3 medium pears; 1¾ cups sliced
Plums	1½–2½	lug 4-basket crate or carton tight-filled carton	18–22 24–32 26–30	8 medium plums; 2 cups halved
Rhubarb	3	carton carton	5 15–20	4–8 stalks; 3 cups sliced; 1 cup cooked
Asparagus	3–3½	half crate or carton pyramid crate	14–15 30–32	16–20 stalks

19

Produce	Pounds (as picked) required to pack quart jar	Volume container	Average weight (pounds) of container	Equivalent measure (per pound)
Beans—Green Snap or Wax	1½	bushel basket, hamper, crate or carton	28–30	3 cups
Beans, Lima	3–5 (2 shelled)	bushel basket or hamper	30	3 cups shelled
Beets	2½–3 (topped)	bag (topped) bag (topped)	25 50	2 cups cooked, sliced
Carrots	2–3 (topped)	carton (bunched) master container of 1-pound bags	23–27 48	8 small carrots; 4 cups chopped
Corn	3–6	wire-bound crate	50	1 ear; (4 ears = 1 cup cut)
Cucumbers	(4 large)	bushel basket, crate or carton	47–55	(1 small = 1 cup sliced)
Greens—Beet, Spinach, etc.	2	16" crate or 1 1/9 bushel crate 1 2/5 or 1 3/5 bushel crate	20–25 30–35	8 cups fresh; 2 cups cooked
Mushrooms	1	4-quart basket	3	40 medium mushrooms; 4 cups sliced
Peas, Green	4–6 (2 shelled)	bushel basket, hamper, 1 1/9 bushel crate	28–30	1 cup shelled, cooked
Pumpkins, Winter Squash	1½–3	bushel crate, 1 1/9 bushel crate or carton	40–45	
Tomatoes	2½–3½	lug carton	20 30	3–4 medium tomatoes; 3 cups sliced or diced

2 PRESERVING METHODS AND EQUIPMENT

PRESERVING METHODS

Open-Kettle

In open-kettle preserving, food is cooked in an uncovered kettle, then transferred, still boiling, into hot sterilized jars. Each jar is sealed immediately after being filled. This method of cooking is only suitable for food in which enzymes and microorganisms are easily destroyed. Therefore, it is only recommended for jams, jellies, conserves, marmalades, relishes and some pickles.

Cold or Raw Pack

In the cold or raw pack method of filling jars, clean hot jars are packed with prepared raw fruit. Hot water, syrup or, in the case of tomatoes, hot tomato juice is added to cover the fruit completely. The jars are sealed and then processed according to recipe directions. This method is only recommended for fruit and tomatoes.

Hot Pack

All vegetables, except tomatoes, must be packed by the hot pack method. The vegetable is precooked for a short time in a covered kettle, then packed into clean hot jars and covered with the boiling cooking liquid or with fresh boiling water. The jar is sealed and processed according to recipe instructions. The hot pack method can also be used for fruit juice, most fruit and tomatoes. This method helps to eliminate enzymes and microorganisms in food that are destroyed at boiling temperature (212°F) before

21

the food is packed into jars. The precooking reduces air in the jars to a minimum and shrinks the food, making it easier to pack more food in the jars. This method also shortens processing time.

PROCESSING

Processing is the term used when food packed in preserving jars is heated to a temperature that will insure destruction of all enzymes and food spoilage microorganisms, so that food will be preserved safely for future use. Food must be subjected to the processing temperature long enough to insure that every bit of food in the container has been brought to the right temperature for complete destruction of spoilage organisms. Food should not be exposed to high temperatures for longer than the recipe directs or it will be overcooked.

There are two methods used for processing: water-bath processing and steam-pressure processing.

Water-Bath Processing

The water bath processes food at a temperature of 212°F (boiling) and therefore is recommended only for fruit, jams, marmalades, preserves, pickles, relishes and tomatoes. Never process low-acid food such as vegetables, meat, poultry or seafood in a boiling-water bath. The spores of *Clostridium botulinum* are not destroyed at 212°F.

Water should be hot, *but not boiling,* when filled jars are lowered into the processor. *Jars are likely to break if put into a processor of boiling water.* More water should be added if needed, to keep the jars covered by one or two inches. The container is then covered and the water is brought to a rolling boil as quickly as possible. Timing for processing begins when the water begins to boil. Water should be kept at a steady boil but not hard enough to shake the jars. Jars are removed from the water-bath as soon as processing time is up.

See Equipment (page 23) for description of water-bath processor.

Steam-Pressure Processing

The steam-pressure processor is especially designed to cook food at very high temperatures for a short length of time. During processing the high temperature (240°F) kills bacteria that are capable of withstanding boiling-water bath temperatures of 212°F. Processing in the steam-pressure processor is the only method recommended for low-acid food such as vegetables, meat, poultry and seafood.

See Equipment (page 24) for description of steam-pressure processor.

EQUIPMENT

Much of the equipment essential for home-preserving can be found in the average kitchen. It is important to check all equipment and be certain it is in good working order before you begin to work. A suggested list of equipment follows—some necessary and all helpful for successful home-preserving. To familiarize you with the larger, more complex pieces of equipment a detailed description and illustrations are provided.

Water-Bath Processor

A water-bath processor or boiling-water bath is really a large kettle, pail, wash boiler or any other container in which water can be boiled. It must be deep enough to cover the largest jar to be used by two inches and still boil briskly without spilling over. (If the water does not cover the containers by at least two inches, food will cook unevenly.) It should have a close fitting lid to prevent excessive evaporation and to conserve fuel. A rack or metal basket should fit in the container and hold the jars to prevent them from touching one another or from touching the bottom or sides of the vessel, and to allow water to circulate freely around them. This piece of equipment can be used as a processor for fruit and tomatoes, or for sterilizing jars to be filled with jams, jellies, marmalades, pickles or relishes.

Steam-Pressure Processor

A steam-pressure processor, essential for the safe processing of vegetables and other low-acid foods, is a large metal kettle with a cover which can be clamped on to make it steam-tight. The cover is equipped with an automatic safety release, or petcock, and with a vent pipe to force out air trapped in the processor when the cover is locked on. The cover also has a steam-pressure gauge, or weights which serve the same purpose. To insure accuracy the pressure gauge should be checked by the manufacturer every year. Failure to do this could result in an incorrect reading, with under processing of food, and with incomplete destruction of the spores of *Clostridium botulinum*.

There are several kinds of pressure cookers on the market and they come in different sizes. Many households own a small pressure cooker for quick preparation of family meals. If your pressure cooker can be used at 240°F (10 lbs. pressure at sea level), it can be used as a processor for preserving jars of low-acid food. However, some pressure cookers are too small to accommodate even the small pint-size jars, so before you start, check to make sure your pressure cooker will accommodate the jars you plan to use. If you are planning to buy a pressure cooker look for a model that has a domed lid especially designed for the homemaker who would like to use this equipment for preserving and for regular preparation of meals. Larger and more expensive pressure cookers are also available. These are called pressure canners, steam-pressure canners and speed-pressure cookers. Before buying one, determine what size jars you will be using and then choose a pressure cooker to accommodate them. Buying a large pressure cooker can be an expensive investment. If you have friends or neighbours who enjoy preserving, perhaps you can team up with them and make the purchase together.

Different manufacturers provide different features in the lid for gauging and controlling the pressure and for safety. It is important that you read the manufacturer's instructions for the use and care of your steam-pressure cooker carefully, and that you understand the directions completely. If you have never used a pressure cooker, practice by preparing two or three meals for the family to help you gain confidence and be at ease with it during the important processing of low-acid food.

Component Parts of Steam-Pressure Processor

Eight- and 16-quart models have "grips" on each side of the cover and pan instead of the long handles found on the 4- and 6-quart models.

Automatic Pressure Control

This is a precision-made, unbreakable, one-piece control for "cooking without looking." You can hear it as it automatically controls cooking at pressure selected—5, 10 or 15 pounds. There are no springs or gadgets to get out of order in this type of control, therefore it never needs calibration or testing for accuracy. Keep control clean by washing in hot soapy water and by rinsing thoroughly.

If you have a pressure gauge dial instead of an automatic pressure control, be certain the gauge is tested each year by the manufacturer to assure accuracy.

Vent Tube

The weight control is placed on the vent tube. It is important that the tube be kept clean and unblocked by food particles. To clean, carefully insert a piece of wire.

Automatic Safety Release

This safety valve will automatically release if the vent tube is blocked or if moisture in the cooker is depleted.

V-Type Self-Sealing Gasket

The gasket automatically seals the cover when the cooker is closed according to directions and is brought up to operating pressure. It is removable for easy cleaning.

Gasket

Remove the gasket for easy cleaning, and replace it when it is worn out.

Cooking Rack

Use rack whenever directions specify.

Basket

The basket holds jars during processing.

Miscellaneous Equipment

Glass preserving jars
Metal lids and screwbands
Wire rack for cooling processed jars
Jar lifter
Wide-mouth jar funnel
Tongs
Paraffin wax—to seal jelly glasses
Double boiler—for melting wax
Grain alcohol for pectin test (nonpoison-
    ous denatured alcohol)
Tea kettle
Jelly bag or cheesecloth—for jelly-making
Blender
Kettle—A large kettle is necessary for
    cooking jams, jellies, preserves, pickles
    and relishes. Do not use copper, zinc,
    galvanized iron or chipped enamel pans
    when making pickles.
Large saucepan—use for blanching fruit
    and vegetables

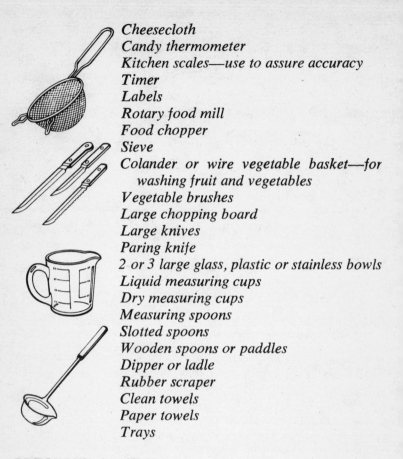

Cheesecloth
Candy thermometer
Kitchen scales—use to assure accuracy
Timer
Labels
Rotary food mill
Food chopper
Sieve
Colander or wire vegetable basket—for washing fruit and vegetables
Vegetable brushes
Large chopping board
Large knives
Paring knife
2 or 3 large glass, plastic or stainless bowls
Liquid measuring cups
Dry measuring cups
Measuring spoons
Slotted spoons
Wooden spoons or paddles
Dipper or ladle
Rubber scraper
Clean towels
Paper towels
Trays

PRESERVING JARS

There are two main requirements for the successful home preservation of food. The first is to allow sufficient processing time at the right temperature in order to destroy all spoilage organisms. The second is to use good quality, modern preserving jars and sealing lids that can be made airtight in order to prevent spoilage organisms from finding their way into the containers after processing.

Considering the expense involved in food preservation, the cost of food and equipment, and the expenditure of time and effort, it is obviously not worth risking food spoilage by trying to cut corners and by using jars not specifically designed for in-home food preservation.

Jars with lids and closures other than those described in this book are also available on the market. But before purchasing them, be sure instructions are included with the jars explaining how to seal them correctly. If lids and rubber rings may be used only once, make certain replacements can be purchased separately.

TYPES OF PRESERVING JARS

Preserving jars come in several shapes and sizes and can be sealed with a variety of fittings.

1

Jelly Tumbler
1. Jelly Tumbler with protective metal cover
   Capacity: 7.5 fluid ounces (about 1 cup)
   The lid is only a protective cover. It cannot be used for any food which requires an airtight seal.

2   3   4

Mason Jars
2. Small Narrow Mouth Mason *Pint*
   Capacity: 16.5 fluid ounces (about 2 cups)
3. Medium Narrow Mouth Mason *Quart*
   Capacity: 32 fluid ounces (about 4 cups)

4. Large Narrow Mouth Mason *One-half gallon*
   Capacity: 60.4 fluid ounces (about 7½ cups)
   The small, medium and large Mason jars are sealed by
   using a flat metal lid and metal screw band or an all-in-
   one metal lid. The jar is self-sealing by vacuum. One size
   lid and screw band fits all three sizes.

5   6   7

Gem Jars

5. Small Gem Jar *Pint*
   Capacity: 16.5 fluid ounces (about 2 cups)
6. Medium Gem Jar *Quart*
   Capacity: 32 fluid ounces (4 cups)
7. Large Gem Jar *One-half gallon*
   Capacity: 60.4 fluid ounces (about 7½ cups)
   The small, medium and large Gem jars are sealed by
   using a flat metal lid and metal screw band, a glass top
   and metal screw band or an all-in-one metal lid. The jars
   are self-sealing by vacuum. One size lid and screw band
   fits all three sizes.

8   9

30

Wide Mouth Mason Jars

8. Small Wide Mouth Mason *Pint*
   Capacity: 16.5 fluid ounces (about 2 cups)
9. Medium Wide Mouth Mason *Quart*
   Capacity: 32.5 fluid ounces (about 4 cups)

The small and medium Wide Mouth Mason jars are sealed by using a metal lid and screw band, a glass top and metal screw band or an all-in-one metal lid. The jars are self-sealing by vacuum. One size lid and screw band fits both jars.

Jars are also identified by size—pint, quart, and half-gallon. This is the U.S. pint measure—2 cups equal 1 pint.

FITTINGS

Flat Metal Lid (used with metal screw band)

These popular lids can be used with Mason, Gem and Wide Mouth Mason Jars. Although they are available in more than one size—one for the small, medium and large Mason and Gem Jars and another size for the small and medium Wide Mouth Mason Jars—they all have the same basic design. The lid edge is lined with a sealing compound. Lids are self-sealing by vacuum.

When purchasing jars, it is not unusual to find the metal lid fitted to the jar with the enamel coated side out. This is done by the manufacturer to prevent damage to the sealing compound. However, when a jar of food is sealed, be sure to place the lid with the enamel side down and the rubber sealing compound against sealing edge of glass.

Lids may be used only once. Screw bands, if in perfect condition, may be reused.

All-in-One Metal Lid

This fitting combines the flat metal lid and the screw band into a one operation closure for Mason, Gem and Wide Mouth Mason Jars. It is self-sealing by vacuum.

Glass Lid
(used with a rubber ring and metal screw band)

These lids are available in sizes to fit Gem and Wide Mouth Mason Jars.

Domed Glass Lid
(used with rubber ring and jar with wire-bail)
These lids come with jars fitted with wire bails which fasten over the lid to create a seal.

Rubber Rings
Rubber rings are available in different widths. Be sure to buy the right size rings to fit your jar. Manufacturers often label boxes of rings with the trade name of the jars on which the rings should be used.

HOW TO SEAL JARS

The jars and fittings described are representative of those most commonly available. If you have a different type of jar or fitting, be sure to follow the manufacturer's instructions for sealing.

Jars with flat metal lids and metal screw bands
1. Fill jar. Wipe rim clean.
2. Put lid on jar with sealing compound next to glass.
3. Screw metal band on tight, by hand. Do not use a wrench.
4. Do not tighten further after processing; this jar is self-sealing.

Jars with glass lids and metal screw bands
1. Fill jar. Wipe rim clean.
2. Fit wet rubber ring on glass lid.
3. Put lid on jar, rubber side down.
4. Screw band on until it is almost tight. Then turn it back nearly a quarter turn. Be absolutely certain jar and band meet.
5. As soon as jars are taken from processor, screw band on tightly.

Jars with domed glass lid, rubber ring, and wire bail
1. Fit rubber ring on ledge at top of jar.
2. Fill jar. Wipe jar rim and rubber ring clean.
3. Put on glass lid to fit into groove. Leave short wire up.
4. After processing, and immediately upon removal from processor, push short wire down to complete seal.

HOW TO STERILIZE JARS

Jars to be filled with food that will not undergo processing in a water-bath or steam-pressure processor, such as some pickles, relishes, jams, jellies and preserves, must be sterilized.

1. Fill a deep water-bath two-thirds full of water. Cover and begin heating on stove. The water-bath should have a wire basket or rack to prevent jars from sitting on the bottom of the pan.
2. Examine all jars with fingertips for nicks, chips or scratches in the sealing edge. These tiny imperfections can cause improper sealing which can be the cause of food spoilage.

3. Jars and lids should be washed in hot suds and rinsed in clear water. Do not use cleansing powder, harsh brushes or scouring pads for cleaning jars. They can damage the glass.
4. Rinse jars and lids well.
5. Sterilize jars by placing them upright in the water-bath. Hold each jar with tongs and allow it to fill with warm water until it can stand alone. When jars are in position, add additional hot water until they are covered by one to two inches of water. Cover water-bath, bring water to a boil and boil twenty minutes.

6. Boil lids five minutes.
7. Remove jars and lids from boiling water *one at a time as needed* for filling and sealing. Removing jars from boiling water and allowing them to stand exposed to the air defeats the entire process of sterilization.
8. To prevent jars from cracking when removed from boiling water, place on a dry wood surface or on several thicknesses of paper toweling.

Note: *All equipment used to fill jars (funnel, dipper or measuring cup, knife) should be clean and should be sterilized in boiling water for twenty minutes before use.*

When food is to be processed in a boiling-water bath or steam-pressure processor, it is not necessary to sterilize jars and lids. Follow steps 1 through 4 and then place jars in hot water until ready to fill. Microorganisms which may cause illness or food spoilage will be destroyed by processing the food in the jars according to the recipe.

COOLING SEALED JARS

1. After processing, remove jars from water-bath or steam-pressure processor and stand upright on a wire rack, wooden board, several thicknesses of paper toweling or dry cloths. Inverting jars may break the seal. Place away from cold drafts, which may crack jars.

2. A popping noise may be heard during the cooling process from jars sealed with metal lids and screw bands or with one-piece metal lids. Don't worry; this indicates that a good vacuum has been reached and that the jar has an airtight seal.
3. Do not make any adjustment to lids after jar has cooled, and do not remove or loosen screw-top metal bands. This may break the seal.

HOW TO TEST FOR SEAL

Vacuum-Type seals: When filled jar is cold, test for seal by pressing center of lid. If lid is down and will not move, jar is sealed.

Other Types of Seals: When filled jar is cold, test for seal by carefully inverting each jar one to two minutes to test for leakage.

Never open a sealed jar after processing. A space at the top of the jar, due to shrinkage of food or loss of liquid during processing, will not affect safe storage. But opening the sealer to add more liquid will expose contents to food spoilage organisms.

If the seal is not airtight, refrigerate food and use within a few days. Foods can be resealed by using new lids and reprocessing for the time stated in recipe. However, this is not recommended because it would overcook the food.

If there is sealing failure with food that will not be harmed by additional cooking and does not require processing (such as some pickles and relishes), food may be returned to a saucepan, brought to a boil, and poured into clean, hot sterilized jars. Then it should be sealed with clean, hot sterilized lids and caps.

Pickles that are packed cold will not give a vacuum seal. However, the high acidity of the food usually prevents food spoilage.

STORING PRESERVED FOOD

1. Wipe jar with damp cloth, taking care not to disturb the screw band.

2. Label and date jar.
3. Store in a cool, dark, dry place where the temperature is as close to 50° or 60°F as possible. Failure to store in the dark may result in a change of colour of stored food. If the storage place cannot be kept dark, wrap each jar in paper or store jars in closed cartons.
4. After one week, recheck each jar. Any sign of leakage indicates food spoilage and, painful though it may be, the food must be discarded.

HOW TO OPEN JARS WITH METAL LIDS

1. Unscrew metal band. If it is stuck, run warm water over it to loosen.
2. Puncture lid with a can opener. Levering the lid with a knife between the metal lid and jar can cause damage to the jar and to any fingers that might get in the way.
3. Lids should be discarded. They should never be used more than once. Rusty, bent, or twisted screw bands should also be discarded.
4. As each jar is emptied, wash and dry it thoroughly and store it in a box in a clean cupboard until needed.

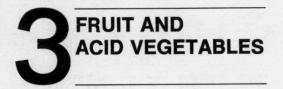

3 FRUIT AND ACID VEGETABLES

When choosing fruit for preserving, care should be taken to select fruit at its peak. It should be fully ripe in order to provide full flavour, but should still be firm, unblemished, and show no sign of spoilage.

Although the acidity of fruit and certain acid vegetables prevents the growth of harmful bacteria, proper methods of preparation and processing are necessary to destroy yeasts and moulds present on the surface that can cause fermentation or mould growth. Heat must be applied to inactivate enzymes, which occur naturally in fruit and bring about ripening changes which, if not stopped, will eventually cause rotting. Enzymes in the presence of oxygen are also responsible for causing colour changes in fruit. Fruit must be processed so that the organisms already present are destroyed. Airtight containers must be used to store fruit in order to prevent recontamination.

Fruit and tomatoes may be safely processed in a boiling-water bath. Follow directions for how to pack jars (cold or hot pack) and processing time precisely.

Altitude Corrections

At sea level water boils at 212°F. As the altitude increases, the temperature at which water boils gradually decreases. The following table gives the number of minutes that should be *added* to the time given in the directions for processing in a boiling-water bath.

Altitude	Increase Water-Bath Processing Time if Time Recommended is:	
	20 minutes or less	More than 20 minutes
1,000 feet	1 minute	2 minutes
2,000 feet	2 minutes	4 minutes
3,000 feet	3 minutes	6 minutes
4,000 feet	4 minutes	8 minutes
5,000 feet	5 minutes	10 minutes
6,000 feet	6 minutes	12 minutes
7,000 feet	7 minutes	14 minutes
8,000 feet	8 minutes	16 minutes
9,000 feet	9 minutes	18 minutes
10,000 feet	10 minutes	20 minutes

Syrups

Fruit to be used for making pie or sauce, or prepared for people who may not eat sugar, can be preserved without the addition of sugar. Sugar is not needed to prevent spoilage. Fruit can be preserved in water, extracted juice or in its own juice. Processing times are the same for unsweetened and sweetened fruit.

However, fruit does have better flavour and colour when preserved in a sugar-water syrup.

Syrups vary in strength from very light to heavy. The choice of syrup depends on type and acidity of the fruit to be preserved, the eventual use of the fruit and personal taste.

Type of Syrup	Sugar	Water	Yield
Very light	1 cup	4 cups	About 4½ cups
Light	1 cup	3 cups	About 3½ cups
Medium	1 cup	2 cups	About 2¼ cups
Heavy	1 cup	1 cup	About 1½ cups

To Make Syrup

Mix sugar and water in a saucepan; bring to a boil over medium heat, stirring occasionally to dissolve sugar. Boil five minutes, skim if necessary. Cover to prevent evaporation and keep hot until used.

Quantity of Syrup to Make

Allow approximately 1½ cups prepared syrup for each quart jar.

Honey and Corn Syrup

Honey or corn syrup can be used to replace up to one-fourth of the sugar in syrup preparation.

Honey has a definite flavour of its own, a factor which must be considered when it is used for preserving. A light flavoured corn syrup is recommended for preserving light-coloured fruit. The addition of 1 teaspoon of lemon juice, or a few grains of salt, to each quart jar of fruit improves the flavour when corn syrup is used.

PREPARATION OF FRUIT

Blanching

To remove the skins of peaches and tomatoes, place them in the top part of a blancher, metal colander or sieve. Immerse in boiling water for 15 to 60 seconds and then immediately dip into cold water. Slip off skins.

To Keep Fruit From Darkening

Light-coloured fruit, such as peaches, pears, apricots and apples, should be dropped, immediately after peeling, into a brine bath made by mixing 1 teaspoon salt with 5 cups cold water. Do not allow fruit to soak more than 20 minutes or it will taste salty. Change the brine when it discolours. Drain and rinse fruit in fresh cold water before packing into jars.

Ascorbic acid (Vitamin C) helps prevent discolouration of light-coloured fruit preserved in glass jars. It is available in powdered, crystalline and tablet form. Place the ascorbic acid in the bottom of the jar before filling with fruit, allowing 1/16 teaspoon (powder or crystals) or 200 milligrams (tablets) for each pint or quart jar. When processing is completed, allow jars to cool; then invert carefully to distribute dissolved ascorbic acid evenly.

HEADSPACE

The space between the surface of the liquid and the rim of the container is the headspace. Leaving proper headspace helps prevent loss of liquid from jars during processing. The amount of space to be allowed at the top of the jar is given in the detailed directions for preserving each food. Most jars of fruit should have a ½-inch headspace.

GENERAL PROCEDURE FOR PRESERVING FRUIT

1. Read through recipe and check to be certain all ingredients and equipment are on hand.
2. Check equipment and utensils for cleanliness and insure that they are in good working order.
3. Fill water-bath processor two thirds full of water, and heat.
4. Check jars for nicks, cracks, and chips on sealing edge. Wash in hot suds; rinse well. Cover with hot water until needed. Wash lids in soapy water and place in saucepan with water. Boil five minutes and keep in hot water until needed.
5. Prepare syrup and cover to prevent evaporation.
6. Sort produce for size, ripeness, and colour. Do not preserve blemished or overripe fruit that shows any sign of decay.
7. Wash fruit well before cutting or removing hulls.
8. Work quickly to keep the time between preparation, packing, and processing to a minimum.
9. Estimate the number of jars the processor can accommodate at one time. Prepare sufficient food for one processing only. Do not prepare and pack food which must be left standing, waiting for processing.
10. Pack jars with food; fill with boiling syrup leaving ½-inch headspace. Pack raw food tightly into container, because it will shrink during processing. Pack hot food fairly loosely.
11. Remove air bubbles by running a clean knife carefully between jar and food. If necessary, add more liquid

to cover food. Be sure to leave headspace recommended in recipe.

12. Wipe top and threads of jar with clean damp cloth or with paper towel.

13. Seal with sterilized lid and screw band (or according to jar manufacturer's instructions).

14. Place jars on rack or in metal basket in water-bath processor. Water should be hot, but not boiling. Add additional hot water to cover jars by one to two inches. Do not pour hot water directly onto jars; this could result in cracking. Cover processor and bring water to a boil. Reduce heat to allow water to boil gently. Begin processing time as water boils and process for length of time given in recipe directions. Maintain water level at one to two inches above the jars by adding additional *boiling* water when necessary.

15. Remove jars from processor and place on a dry wooden board, several thicknesses of paper toweling, or on dry cloths. Place jars a few inches apart, out of drafts, to cool. Adjust lids according to manufacturer's instructions. When cold, test for seal (page 35).

16. If jar has failed to seal it may be repacked, using a new lid and reprocessed as the recipe directs. However, since this can result in badly overcooked food it is preferable to refrigerate and use the food as soon as possible.

17. Wipe jars with damp cloth. Label, indicating contents and date packed.

18. Store in a cool, dark, dry place.

PRESERVING FRUIT WITHOUT SUGAR

Firm Fruit—Apples, Peaches, Pears, etc.

Wash, drain, and prepare fruit. Drop light-coloured fruit into a brine bath to prevent discolouration. Cover the bottom of a pan with ¼ to ½ inch of water, enough to prevent sticking or to make a sauce. Precook five minutes. Pack into hot jars, leaving ½-inch headspace. Cover contents with boiling water or fruit juice, leaving ½-inch headspace. Seal and process according to instructions given for specific fruit in recipe chart.

Juicy Fruit—Berries, Cherries, Currants and Plums

Wash, drain, and prepare fruit for cooking. Either add a small amount of water to pan to prevent sticking or crush a little fruit in pan. Add prepared fruit and simmer until heated through, about 2 to 4 minutes. Pack into hot jars, leaving ½-inch headspace. Fill jars with extracted fruit juice or boiling water, leaving ½-inch headspace. Seal and process according to instructions given for specific fruit in recipe chart.

PROCESSING FRUIT IN A STEAM-PRESSURE PROCESSOR

Fruit and acid vegetables are usually processed in a water bath. However, if you have a steam-pressure processor, all these foods, except strawberries, can be processed under pressure for a much shorter time than is required in a water bath. Care must be taken to time processing accurately because fruit is easily overcooked. Use the cold pack method.

Process firm fruit—apples, cherries, pears, plums, peaches, tomatoes—for 10 minutes at five pounds pressure. Process juicy fruit and berries, except strawberries, for eight minutes at five pounds pressure. Timing is the same for pint and quart jars.

STATEMENT ON TOMATOES

Recently new varieties of tomatoes have appeared on the market which are not acid enough to be safely canned in the boiling water bath. As it is difficult for the home canner to identify these new varieties it is now considered a necessary safety precaution to add a small amount of acid when canning tomatoes. Citric acid is the principal acid found in tomatoes. When dissolved in water and added to each jar of tomatoes in the amounts recommended on page 45, citric acid raises the acidity of tomatoes to a level whereby they may be safely canned in a boiling water bath. Citric acid is easily available in drugstores.

Fruit	Syrup to Use	Pack	Preparing and Packing	Processing Time in Minutes Boiling-Water Bath* Pint Jars	Quart Jars
Apples	Light or Medium	Hot	Wash, peel, and core. Quarter, or cut in 1/4-inch rings. Drop into brine bath. Drain and rinse. Bring to a boil in syrup and simmer 3 minutes. Pack hot. Leave 1/2-inch headspace. Cover with boiling syrup, leaving 1/2-inch headspace. Seal and process. Red food colouring may be added to colour syrup and fruit.	20	20
Applesauce	Sweeten to taste (about 1/4 cup sugar to 4 or 5 apples).	Hot	Wash, peel, core, and quarter. Simmer, covered until tender, in a small amount of water to prevent sticking. Press through sieve. Add clove and cinnamon. Sweeten if desired. Pour hot into hot jars leaving 1/2-inch headspace. Seal and process.	15	20
Apricots	Medium or Heavy	Hot	Wash, halve and pit fruit. Drop into brine bath. Drain and rinse. Bring to a boil in syrup and simmer 2 to 3 minutes. Pack hot, cut side down, leaving 1/2-inch headspace. Cover with boiling syrup, leaving 1/2-inch headspace. Seal and process.	20	25
		Cold	Wash, halve and pit, or leave whole. Drop into brine bath. Drain and rinse. Pack cut side down if halved, leaving 1/2-inch headspace. Cover with boiling syrup, leaving 1/2-inch headspace. Seal and process.	25	30
Blueberries Blackberries Raspberries Gooseberries	Light Medium Medium to Heavy Heavy	Cold	Wash and prepare fruit. Remove blossom and stem ends. Pack, leaving 1/2-inch headspace. Cover with boiling syrup, leaving 1/2-inch headspace. Seal and process.	15	20

43

Fruit	Syrup to Use	Pack	Preparing and Packing	Processing Time in Minutes Boiling-Water Bath*	
				Pint Jars	Quart Jars
Sweet cherries Sour cherries	Medium Medium to Heavy	Hot	Wash, stem, and pit if desired. Bring to a boil in syrup and simmer 3 minutes. Pack hot, leaving ½-inch headspace. Seal and process.	15	15
		Cold	Wash, stem, and pit if desired. Pack, leaving ½-inch headspace. Cover with boiling syrup, leaving ½-inch headspace. Seal and process.	20	25
Peaches	Medium	Hot	Blanch 50 to 60 seconds. Cold dip. Remove skins. Halve, pit and drop into brine bath. Drain and rinse. Leave in halves or slice. Bring to a boil in syrup and simmer 3 minutes. Pack hot, cups down if halved, leaving ½-inch headspace. Cover with boiling syrup, leaving ½-inch headspace. Add ascorbic acid if desired. Seal and process.	15	15
		Cold	Blanch 50 to 60 seconds. Cold dip. Remove skins. Halve, pit, and drop into brine bath. Drain and rinse. Leave in halves or slice. Pack, cups down if halved, leaving ½-inch headspace. Cover with boiling syrup, leaving ½-inch headspace. Add ascorbic acid if desired. Seal and process.	20	25
Pears	Light Spices, flavouring and food colouring may be added to syrup if desired	Hot	Wash, peel, halve or quarter. Remove core. Drop into brine bath. Drain and rinse. Bring to a boil in syrup and simmer tender fleshed varieties 3 minutes, firm fleshed varieties 5 minutes. Pack hot, leaving ½-inch headspace. Cover with boiling syrup, leaving ½-inch headspace. Seal and process.	15	15

Food	Syrup	Pack	Directions		
Sour plums Prune plums	Medium to Heavy Light to Medium	Hot	Wash, leave whole, or halve and pit. Bring to a boil in syrup and simmer 2 minutes. Pack hot, leaving ½-inch headspace. Cover with boiling syrup, leaving ½-inch headspace. Seal and process.	15	15
		Cold	Wash, leave whole, or halve and pit. Pack, leaving ½-inch headspace. Cover with boiling syrup, leaving ½-inch headspace. Seal and process.	20	25
Rhubarb	Heavy	Cold	Wash and cut into ½-inch pieces. Pack, leaving ½-inch headspace. Cover with boiling syrup, leaving ½-inch headspace. Seal and process.	10	15
Strawberries	Heavy	Hot	Wash and hull. Bring syrup to a boil in kettle. Add strawberries. Cover, remove from heat, let stand 1 hour. Bring to a boil. Pack hot, leaving ½-inch headspace. Seal and process.	10	10
		Cold	Wash and hull. Bring slowly to a boil in syrup. Cover, remove from heat, let stand 1 hour. Bring to a boil. Pack, leaving ½-inch headspace. Seal and process.	15	20
Tomatoes	None	Cold	Blanch 15 to 60 seconds. Cold dip. Remove stem ends and peel. Half-fill containers with tomatoes. Add ¼ teaspoon citric acid and ½ teaspoon salt dissolved in 1 tablespoon boiling water to each pint jar. Add ½ teaspoon citric acid and 1 teaspoon salt dissolved in 1 tablespoon boiling water to each quart jar. Finish filling jars. Cover tomatoes with hot tomato juice or water, leaving ½-inch headspace. Seal and process. (Citric acid is available at drugstores.)	55	60

*Processing times given are for foods processed at altitudes less than 1,000 feet above sea level. See page 38 for additional processing time required at higher altitudes.

Brandied Fruit
Makes 1 large crock

1 bottle (32 to 40 ounces) brandy
Grated rind of 1 large orange
Grated rind of 1 lemon
Grated rind of 1 lime
Grated rind of ¼ grapefruit
1 cinnamon stick
1 whole nutmeg
12 whole cloves
6 whole allspice
1 quart ripe, perfect strawberries, washed and hulled

Sugar
Sweet cherries, stemmed, washed & pitted
Ripe peaches, peeled, pitted and quartered
Ripe pineapple, pared, cored and cubed
Blackberries or raspberries, washed and stemmed

Wash a large earthenware crock and rinse thoroughly with boiling water. Pour in brandy. Add grated rinds and spices. Weigh strawberries and weigh out exactly the same amount of sugar. Add strawberries and sugar to the crock. Place a plate on top of the fruit to hold under the brandy. Cover crock tightly and let stand in a cool place.

Add cherries, peaches, pineapple and berries in desired quantities as they become available during the season. Each time new fruit is added, weigh it and add to crock with an equal weight of sugar. Keep fruit submerged in brandy-syrup by weighting down with plate.

When last fruit has been added, cover crock very tightly and let stand in a cool place 3 months before using any fruit. After fruit mixture has fermented 3 months, it can be packed in hot sterilized jars and sealed. Or it can be left covered in the crock in a cool place.

Brandied Peaches

Makes about 3 quarts

1 basket (4 quarts, about
   5 pounds) ripe peaches
3 cups sugar
1 cup brandy

1 orange, sliced
Cinnamon sticks
Whole cloves

Wash peaches. Blanch 40 to 60 seconds in boiling water. Plunge into cold water and slip off skins. Leave small peaches whole. Halve and pit large peaches. Drop peaches into a brine bath to prevent discolouration. Combine sugar and 1½ cups water in a kettle and bring to a boil, stirring to dissolve sugar. Cover mixture and keep hot. Pack drained peaches into clean, hot pint or quart jars to ½ inch from sealing edge (eight or nine small whole peaches to a quart jar). Add two or three orange slices, one cinnamon stick, and 3 or 4 whole cloves to each jar. Stir brandy into hot syrup and pour over fruit in jars, leaving ½-inch headspace. Wipe top and threads of jars and seal. Process pint jars for 20 minutes in a boiling-water bath, process quart jars for 25 minutes.

Chestnuts in Rum

Makes about 3 pints

2 pounds fresh chestnuts
4½ cups dark brown sugar
1½ cups light rum

½ orange, cut into thin slices
1 tablespoon chopped
   candied ginger

Bring 6 cups of water to a boil in a saucepan. Add chestnuts and simmer, covered, about 1 hour or until tender. Drain. Remove skins and rinse thoroughly. Combine brown sugar, 1½ cups water, rum, seeded orange slices and ginger. Heat until sugar is dissolved. Pack chestnuts into hot sterilized jars. Pour syrup over chestnuts. Include 1 orange slice per jar. Seal immediately.

4 VEGETABLES

Do not even *consider* preserving vegetables unless you have a steam-pressure processor in good working order, capable of accommodating small or medium-size jars. *To insure complete destruction of harmful microorganisms capable of withstanding high temperatures in low-acid food (vegetables, meat, poultry and seafood), processing must be done in a steam-pressure processor capable of 10 pounds of pressure (240°F) at sea level for the correct length of time directed in up-to-date recipes.* We cannot stress the importance of this too strongly. Some people may bring up the fact that in past years processing of *all* food in jars or cans was done in a water-bath processor only capable of reaching boiling water temperature, 212°F. But they forget to add that the people who did not encounter *botulin* poison when processing by this method were just plain lucky!

Home-preservers who ignore recommendations that are based on recent laboratory findings, or who turn to older publications with out-dated information, are flirting with danger—and even with their lives.

If the microorganism *Clostridium botulinum,* capable of withstanding a temperature of 212°F (boiling water at sea level) in low-acid food, is not destroyed it will, during storage of food, produce *botulin* poison which may be un-noticeable by smell, taste, or appearance. *It is fatal in very small doses.*

SELECTING VEGETABLES

When choosing vegetables for preserving, take care to select young, tender vegetables that show no sign of spoilage. Vegetables should be preserved as soon as possible after being picked.

PROCESSING TIME

Follow recommended processing times carefully. Each time given applies to a specific food, prepared according to specific instructions. Processing times are based on the time it takes for heat to penetrate the food so that every particle reaches 240°F at sea level. The same vegetable, cut differently, requires different processing times. For example, whole-kernel corn packed in small jars and processed at 10 pounds pressure requires 60 minutes of processing, but cream-style corn, packed in the same size jar and processed at the same pressure, must be processed for 75 minutes. So follow processing times given in recipes exactly.

Altitude Corrections

If you live at an altitude of less than 2,000 feet above sea level, process vegetables at 10 pounds of pressure for the time given in recipe. If you live at an altitude above 2,000 feet, it takes more than 10 pounds of pressure to reach 240°F. Process according to the following table.

Altitude	Pounds of Pressure	Processing Time
2,000 feet	11 pounds	As recipe recommends
4,000 feet	12 pounds	As recipe recommends
6,000 feet	13 pounds	As recipe recommends
8,000 feet	14 pounds	As recipe recommends
10,000 feet	15 pounds	As recipe recommends

If your gauge is weighted, use 15 pounds of pressure for processing done at altitudes over 2,000 feet.

SALT

Salt is used in vegetable preservation for flavour only. It does not aid in preservation. Add ½ teaspoon of salt to each pint jar, and 1 teaspoon of salt to each quart jar.

HEADSPACE

Leave a ½-inch headspace in jars, with the exception of jars packed with corn or peas. They expand more than other vegetables during processing and therefore require 1-inch headspace.

HOT PACK METHOD

The hot pack method must be used for all vegetables except tomatoes. This method helps to inactivate enzymes and microorganisms destroyed at boiling-water temperatures. It also reduces air in the jars to a minimum and shrinks food, making it easier to pack more food into jars, and shortens processing time.

Sort, wash, drain and prepare vegetables as recipe directs. Cover with boiling water, return to boil, cover, and boil for the time recommended in the recipe. Pack hot mixture in clean hot jars. Add salt. Cover with hot cooking liquid up to recommended headspace. Cover with additional *boiling* water if needed. Seal and process immediately according to instructions given for specific vegetable in recipe chart.

Do not prepare more jars than your steam-pressure processor can handle at one time.

ON GUARD AGAINST SPOILAGE

Don't taste or eat vegetables that show signs of spoilage. Check each container carefully before using it. Bulging jar lids or rings, or a leak, may mean the seal has broken and the food has spoiled. When you open a container check for other warning signs—spurting liquid, strange odour, or mold.

Botulin toxin is difficult to detect by appearance, smell or taste. Therefore, as a precautionary measure, it is recommended that all home-processed vegetables and preserving liquid be boiled 10 minutes in an open sauce-pan before being tasted or eaten. Boiling for this length of time destroys the toxin.

Burn spoiled vegetables or dispose of the food in such a way that it can not be eaten by either humans or animals.

GENERAL PROCEDURE
FOR PRESERVING VEGETABLES

1. Read recipes all the way through. Make sure equipment and ingredients necessary are available.
2. Read instruction booklet that accompanies steam-pressure processor.
3. Check jars for nicks, cracks, and chips on sealing edge. Discard jars that are not perfect. Wash jars and lids in hot suds. Rinse jars well and leave in hot water until needed. Boil lids five minutes. Remove from hot water one at a time as needed.
4. Sort produce for size. Don't preserve vegetables showing signs of spoilage.
5. Wash vegetables well before peeling or cutting. Use a vegetable brush to remove soil.
6. Estimate the number of jars the processor can accommodate at one time. Prepare sufficient food for one processing only. Don't soak vegetables in water before bottling or valuable minerals and vitamins may be lost.
7. Place vegetables in a kettle and cover with boiling water. Bring to a boil, cover, and boil for the time recommended in the recipe.
8. To prevent hot, empty jars from cracking, place on a dry cloth or wooden board.
9. Work as quickly as possible when packing vegetables into jars.
10. Fill jars, one at a time, with vegetables. Add salt and cover with boiling cooking liquid or with boiling water. Remember to leave the recommended headspace.
11. When jars are filled, work out air bubbles by running

the blade of a clean knife inside the jar between food and jar.

12. Seal each jar with a sterilized lid and screw band as it is filled.

13. Place filled, sealed jars in steam-pressure processor. Follow the manufacturer's instructions for use of processor. Process at the pressure given in the recipe for the recommended length of time.

14. After processing, follow instructions for opening processor. Remove jars from processor and place on a wire rack or folded cloth. To prevent cracking, don't place hot jars on cold or wet surfaces. Keep jars out of drafts while cooling.

15. Adjust lids according to manufacturer's instructions.

16. When cold, test for seal (page 35).

17. If jar has failed to seal, food may be repacked, boiling hot, in clean, hot jars, sealed with a new lid, and reprocessed according to directions in original recipe. Never allow more than 24 hours to elapse before reprocessing. However, as reprocessing can result in badly overcooked food, you may prefer to refrigerate and use as soon as possible.

18. Wipe jars. Label, indicating contents and date packed.

19. Store in a cool, dark, dry place.

CAUTION

Check to be certain your steam-pressure processor is in perfect working order before you preserve vegetables. Follow recipes and processing times precisely. As an added safeguard, boil all home-preserved vegetables, except tomatoes, with their liquid, uncovered, for at least 10 minutes before tasting or eating. Corn and squash should be boiled 20 minutes.

Do not taste or eat any vegetable that foams or has an unusual or unpleasant odour. Burn or dispose of spoiled vegetables in such a way that they cannot be eaten by humans or animals.

RECIPE TABLE FOR STEAM-PRESSURE PROCESSED VEGETABLES
PROCESSED AT 10 POUNDS PRESSURE

Vegetable	Preparing and Packing	Required Processing Time in Minutes*	
		Pint Jars	Quart Jars
Asparagus	Wash, break off tough ends of stalks. Remove scales if necessary to wash away sand. Cut into lengths to fit containers, and still provide required ½-inch headspace. Tie in uniform bundles. Stand upright in sufficient boiling water to cover half the stalks. Cover, bring to a boil, and boil 3 minutes. Pack hot, tips up, (a few stalks inverted in center will help keep stalks upright). Add salt. Cover with hot cooking liquid leaving ½-inch headspace. Seal and process.	30	35
Beans—Green or Wax	Wash young tender beans. Trim ends and remove strings if necessary. Leave whole or cut in pieces. Cover with boiling water. Bring to a boil and boil, covered, 3 minutes. Pack hot, leaving ½-inch headspace. Add salt. Cover with hot cooking liquid leaving ½-inch headspace. Seal and process.	30	35
Beets	Wash small young beets. Leave on roots and 2 inches of stem to prevent bleeding. Cover with boiling water. Bring to a boil and boil, covered, until skins slip off easily, about 25 minutes. Remove skins, stems and roots. Pack hot, leaving ½-inch headspace. Add salt. Cover with boiling water, leaving ½-inch headspace. Seal and process.	30	35
Carrots	Wash and scrape tender young carrots. Cover with boiling water. Bring to a boil and boil, covered, 5 minutes. Pack hot in upright position alternating stem and root ends. Leave ½-inch headspace. Add salt. Cover with boiling water, leaving ½-inch headspace. Seal and process.	30	35

Corn, Whole-Kernel	Wash ears. Cover with boiling water. Bring to a boil and boil, covered, 4 minutes. Dip into cold water. Cut whole kernels from cobs. Cover with boiling water, using half as much water as corn. Bring to a boil. Pack hot, very loosely, leaving 1-inch headspace. Add salt. Seal and process.	60	70
Corn, Cream-Style	Wash ears. Slice thin layer from kernels off cob. Next, slice remainder of kernels from cob and finally scrape cob to remove cream or juice. Cover with boiling water, using half as much water as corn. Bring to boil, stirring to prevent scorching. Pack hot, very loosely, leaving 1-inch headspace. Add salt. Seal and process.	75	Not recommended
Greens—Spinach, Chard, Beet Tops	Wash thoroughly. Cook, covered, in very little water until completely wilted, about 5 to 8 minutes. Turn several times during cooking. Pack hot, very loosely, leaving ½-inch headspace. Cut greens crosswise to bottom of container with a sharp clean knife. Add salt. Cover with boiling water, leaving ½-inch headspace. Seal and process.	50	60
Mushrooms	Do not home process mushrooms.		
Peas	Shell and wash young tender peas. Cover with boiling water. Bring to a boil and boil, covered, 1 minute. Pack hot, very loosely, leaving 1-inch headspace. Add salt. Cover with hot cooking liquid, leaving 1-inch headspace. Seal and process.	40	45
Pumpkins, Winter Squash	Cut or break apart. Remove seeds and stringy fibers. Cut into pieces. Steam, bake or boil in small amount of water, until tender. Scrape meat from skins and mash or put through a sieve. Bring to a boil, adding a little water, if necessary, to prevent scorching. Pack hot, leaving ½-inch headspace. Seal and process.	70	80

*Processing pressure and times given are for foods processed at altitudes less than 2,000 feet above sea level. See page 49 for directions on processing at higher altitudes.

5 JAMS, PRESERVES, CONSERVES, MARMALADES AND BUTTERS

There is something very special about being able to serve homemade spreads and offer a variety of jams, jellies and conserves. Jams and jellies are best when made in small batches and therefore often can be made in one leisurely afternoon. Although supermarkets stock an endless variety of jams and jellies, few can match the delicious full flavour of those made at home.

Jam is made from fruit that has been left whole, cut up or crushed. The fruit is cooked to soften the skin and cell structure, and to extract the pectin. It is then boiled with sugar to form a gel and used as a spread.

Preserves are made from small whole fruit or larger fruit, cut into equal-size pieces and cooked in a syrup solution. When fruit is not cut, care should be taken to retain the natural shape of the fruit. It is often recommended that cooked fruit be allowed to sit overnight to provide time for syrup to penetrate the fruit. The fruit is then packed in jars and the syrup is boiled to the desired density. A soft gel results. Preserves are used as toppings for ice cream, cake, dessert, or as spreads.

Conserves are often made from a combination of fruits to which nuts and raisins may be added. They are usually less sweet than jams. The nuts should be dipped in boiling water and added during the last five minutes of cooking. Conserves are used as toppings, spreads, and cake fillings.

Marmalades can be made from a mixture of fruits, one of which is usually a citrus fruit. They are delicious served for breakfast with bread, rolls, or sweet rolls.

Butters are made from cooked fruit pulp. Sweet or spicy, they make fine spreads.

ACID

Acid is essential in making jam and jelly. When heated with sugar and pectin, the juice changes into a semisolid. Fruit is more acid when slightly underripe. A recipe may be supplemented with lemon juice or tartaric acid to increase the acid content of the mixture.

SUGAR

The amount of sugar added to a recipe depends on the amount of pectin. A high pectin content permits more sugar to be added to the recipe. This can improve the flavour and prolong the shelf life of filled jars.

NATURAL PECTIN

Pectin is a substance which occurs naturally in fruit. When heated in the presence of acid and sugar in the right proportions a gel results. Different fruit contain different amounts of pectin. The same fruit can vary from year to year in the amount of pectin it contains.

Slightly underripe fruit contain more pectin than ripe fruit. In overripe fruit the pectin is converted to pectic acid and loses its jelling power.

Ripe fruit offers the best flavour for jam or jelly, but the jelling power is low. Therefore, to obtain a jam that is high in flavour and gels well, a mixture of ripe and slightly underripe fruit is often used in a recipe. Since overcooking also destroys the jelling power, follow recipe instructions exactly.

COMMERCIAL PECTIN

Pectin can be added to a recipe through the use of a commercial pectin or by adding juice made from a fruit high in pectin, such as apples. When using commercial pectin, care should be taken to follow the package instructions exactly. Liquid pectin comes in 6-ounce bottles. Pectin in powder form comes in 1¾-ounce envelopes, usually one envelope to each box. Always use the type of pectin called for in the recipe.

PECTIN AND ACID CONTENT OF FRUIT

Fruit High in Pectin and High in Acid: Sour apples, red and black currants, gooseberries, crabapples, cranberries, grapefruit, lemons, limes, grapes, blackberries, sour cherries, sour guavas, loganberries, sour oranges and most varieties of plums.

Fruit High in Pectin and Low in Acid: Sweet apples, sweet guavas, quinces, melons, bananas, sweet cherries and unripe figs.

Fruit Low in Pectin and High in Acid: Apricots, rhubarb, strawberries, pineapples, pomegranates and sweet cherries.

Fruit Low in Pectin and Low in Acid: Pears, peaches, ripe figs, raspberries, elderberries and overripe fruit.

Testing for Pectin Content

A test can be made to determine the pectin content of fruit cooked in water. Mix 1 tablespoon of cooked fruit juice with 1 tablespoon of grain alcohol (nonpoisonous denatured) and stir slowly. The alcohol precipitates the pectin and forms a clot. The type of clot formed indicates the quantity of pectin.

Those fruits that have low pectin content should have pectin added. Many recipes combine fruits high in pectin with those low in pectin to obtain interesting flavour combinations and still provide a good gel.

JAM OR GEL STAGE

Fruit is cooked with or without sugar to soften the fruit and extract the pectin. Sugar is added (if not added in the beginning) and the mixture is boiled rapidly to evaporate excess moisture and bring the jelly to the right stage for jelling. This gel stage can be determined several ways. Caution: To be certain gel stage is not missed, remove jam from heat during testing.

Temperature Test

Most fruit reaches the jam or gel stage between 221°F and 230°F. Therefore a jelly or candy thermometer can be helpful in determining when the gel stage has been reached. Fruit that is rich in pectin may reach the gel stage at about 218°F.

Another way to test for gel stage is to take the temperature of boiling water in your area. Gel stage is usually reached at 8°F above the temperature of boiling water.

Take temperature reading carefully. Stir mixture thoroughly and make certain the thermometer does not touch the bottom of the kettle.

Drop Test

The gel stage is difficult to determine when the mixture is hot. Therefore, the jam must be removed from the heat for each test. Dip a chilled metal spoon into the jam and allow it to drip from the spoon. When two drops run together to form one, the gel stage has been reached.

Plate Test

Drop a little jam onto a chilled plate and cool quickly. When the gel stage has been reached, jam should crinkle slightly when pushed.

SCUM

A scum may form over the surface of jam during cooking. It should be removed just before jam is poured into jars. Continual skimming during cooking is wasteful.

FILLING JARS

After the jam has reached the gel stage, remove from heat. Skim and pour quickly into hot sterilized jelly glasses or preserving jars, leaving about ½-inch headspace. Marmalades or jams that contain whole fruit should be allowed to cool slightly, then stirred gently to distribute the fruit. This will keep it suspended in the jam and prevent it from rising to the surface.

JELLY GLASSES OR PRESERVING JARS

Jams, jellies, marmalades, and conserves can be stored in jelly glasses or in preserving jars. However, preserves should only be sealed in preserving jars.

Preparation of Jars
1. Check jars for nicks, cracks or sharp edges.
2. Wash carefully in hot suds and rinse well.
3. Sterilize in boiling water 20 minutes. Leave in hot water until needed.
4. Remove jars, and place upside down on a wooden board or several thicknesses of paper toweling.
5. Jars should be hot when filled.
6. Protective caps or metal lids should be boiled five minutes and left in the water until needed.

SEALING

Jams, jellies, marmalades, and conserves can be sealed with hot, melted paraffin wax, or with a metal lid and screw band. Preserves should only be sealed with the metal lid and screw band.

Paraffin Wax

Melt paraffin wax in top part of a double boiler. Paraffin should be hot but not smoking.

Allow jam to cool slightly. For a perfect seal there should be no dribbles of jam on the inside of the glass above the jam. Pour a thin layer of paraffin over jam, then tilt the jar to make sure the paraffin seals well. Prick any air bubbles that form. When wax is hard, pour a second layer of paraffin over the first layer and tilt the jar to seal. Cover with metal lid and store in a cool, dry place.

GENERAL PROCEDURE FOR MAKING JAM

1. Read through recipe and make sure all ingredients and equipment are on hand.
2. Check jars for nicks and cracks, wash in hot suds, and sterilize in boiling water 20 minutes.
3. Select fruit. Use a mixture of approximately half ripe and half slightly underripe fruit. Wash fruit. Cut away bruised spots.
4. Prepare recipe. Don't double recipes. Best results are obtained when small batches (approximately 3 to 4 quarts of fruit) are prepared at a time.
5. Stir mixture occasionally, especially during final cooking stages, to prevent sticking and scorching.
6. As mixture begins to thicken, test for jam or gel stage. Remember to remove kettle from heat during each test or the correct jam stage may be missed.
7. Fruit rich in pectin, such as gooseberries, black currants and some plums, thicken more as they cool. Therefore, care should be taken not to cook these fruits to a consistency that is too thick (approximately 218°F is adequate).
8. Skim mixture carefully. Pour into hot sterilized jars. Seal immediately if using preserving jars.
9. If using jelly glasses, allow to cool slightly before sealing with paraffin.
10. Fit on protective metal cap.
11. Label, indicating contents and date.
12. Store in a cool, dry place.

Berry Jam
Makes about 4 eight-ounce glasses

4 cups crushed berries　　　　**4 cups sugar**
　(about 2 quarts)

Sort, wash, stem or hull, and drain berries. Crush and measure. Place in kettle, mix thoroughly with sugar. Bring to boil and boil, stirring constantly, until sugar dissolves and gel stage is reached. Remove from heat and skim off foam. Pour hot mixture into hot sterilized glasses and seal immediately.

Note: *This recipe can be used for blackberries, blueberries, boysenberries, gooseberries, loganberries, raspberries and strawberries.*

Plum-Raspberry Jam
Makes about 12 eight-ounce glasses

4 cups plum pulp　　　　　　**10 cups sugar**
　(about 2½ pounds plums)　　**½ cup lemon juice**
3 cups fresh raspberries　　　**1 bottle (6 ounces) liquid pectin**
　(about 1½ pints)

Wash and sort plums and raspberries. Cut plums in half and remove pits. Put through food chopper using fine blade. Place plums and raspberries in large kettle. Add sugar and lemon juice and stir until well blended. Bring mixture to a boil over high heat, stirring constantly. Boil hard 1 minute. Remove from heat and stir in pectin immediately. Skim off foam. Pour hot mixture into hot sterilized glasses and seal immediately.

Currant Jam
Makes 4 or 5 eight-ounce glasses

1 pound currants　　　　　　**4 cups sugar**

Wash currants and remove stems. Place fruit in kettle with 2½ cups water. Bring to a boil and boil, uncovered, 20 minutes, stirring occasionally. Add sugar and stir until dissolved. Return to a boil and cook until gel stage is reached. Remove from heat and skim off foam. Pour hot mixture into hot sterilized glasses and seal immediately.

Fresh Apricot Jam
Makes about 8 eight-ounce glasses

4 pounds fresh apricots   **Juice of 1 lemon**
6 cups sugar

Wash, pit and dice apricots. Do not remove skin. Combine with sugar and lemon juice in a large kettle. Bring to a boil, stirring to dissolve sugar. Boil, uncovered, stirring occasionally, until gel stage is reached. Remove from heat and skim off foam. Pour hot mixture into hot sterilized glasses and seal immediately.

Dried Apricot-Pineapple Jam
Makes about 10 eight-ounce glasses

4 pounds dried apricots, diced   **6 cups sugar**
1 large fresh pineapple or   **Juice of 1 lemon**
   1 can (20 ounces) crushed
   pineapple, well drained

Soak apricots overnight in just enough water to cover. Simmer in a large kettle, uncovered, without draining, 20 minutes. Pare pineapple, remove eyes, core, and grate or chop in blender. Add pineapple, sugar and lemon juice to apricots. Bring to a boil, stirring to dissolve sugar. Boil, uncovered, stirring occasionally, until gel stage is reached. Remove from heat and skim off foam. Pour hot mixture into hot sterilized glasses and seal immediately.

Rhubicot Jam
Makes 5 or 6 eight-ounce glasses

3 cups diced fresh apricots   **1 tablespoon grated orange rind**
   (about 1¼ pounds)   **¼ cup lemon juice**
1 cup diced rhubarb   **2½ cups sugar**
   (about 1 pound)

Wash, pit and dice apricots. Do not peel. Wash, trim off ends, and dice rhubarb. Combine all ingredients in a large kettle, and bring to a boil. Boil, uncovered, stirring occasionally, until gel stage is reached, about 35 to 40 minutes. Remove from heat and skim off foam. Pour hot mixture into hot sterilized glasses and seal immediately.

Strawberry-Rhubarb Jam
Makes about 7 eight-ounce glasses

1 quart strawberries
1½ pounds rhubarb

Juice and grated rind of 1 orange
6 cups sugar

Sort, wash, and hull fully ripe berries. Drain well. Wash rhubarb, trim off ends and cut into ½-inch pieces. Place strawberries, rhubarb, orange juice and rind in a large kettle. Bring to a boil. Add sugar and stir until dissolved. Boil, stirring constantly, until gel stage is reached. Remove from heat and skim off foam. Pour hot mixture into hot sterilized glasses and seal immediately.

Peach-Cantaloupe Jam
Makes 3 to 4 eight-ounce glasses

2 cups diced peaches
  (4 medium peaches)
2 cups diced cantaloupe
  (1 small melon)

Juice and grated rind
  of 2 lemons
3 cups sugar

Wash, blanch and peel, pit and dice peaches. Pare cantaloupe, remove seeds, and dice. Combine all ingredients in a kettle. Bring to a boil and boil, uncovered, stirring occasionally, until gel stage is reached. Remove from heat and skim off foam. Pour hot mixture into hot sterilized glasses and seal immediately.

Plum-Peach Jam
Makes about 9 eight-ounce glasses

5 cups red plums
  (about 3 pounds)
4 cups peaches (about 3 pounds)

8 cups sugar
1 lemon, sliced thin,
  seeds removed

Sort, wash, and drain fruit. Pit plums. Blanch, peel and pit peaches. Cut fruit into small pieces. Combine all ingredients in a kettle and mix thoroughly. Bring to a rapid boil over high heat, and boil, stirring constantly, until mixture thickens and gel stage is reached. Remove from heat and skim off foam. Pour hot mixture into hot sterilized glasses and seal immediately.

Eight Minute Strawberry Jam

Makes 3 or 4 eight-ounce glasses

4 cups sliced strawberries
(about 3 pints)

½ lemon, thinly sliced
4 cups sugar

Wash, hull and slice strawberries. Wash and slice lemon and remove seeds. Combine fruit and sugar in a kettle. Place over low heat, uncovered, until sugar is dissolved. Increase heat and bring to a boil. Boil rapidly until gel stage is reached. Remove from heat and skim off foam. Allow to stand 1 minute. Pour hot mixture into hot sterilized glasses and seal immediately.

Peach Jam

Makes 6 or 7 eight-ounce glasses

6 cups sliced peaches
(12 medium peaches)

3 cups sugar
1 tablespoon lemon juice

Wash, blanch, peel, core and slice peaches. Combine all ingredients and let stand, uncovered, 1 hour. Place in kettle and simmer until sugar is dissolved, stirring constantly. Bring to a boil and boil rapidly until gel stage is reached. Remove from heat and skim off foam. Pour hot mixture into hot sterilized glasses and seal immediately.

Cherry Jam

Makes about 9 eight-ounce glasses

4½ cups chopped sour cherries
(about 3 pounds or
2 quart boxes)
7 cups sugar

1 bottle (6 ounces) liquid pectin
3 teaspoons almond extract
(optional)

Sort, wash, stem, pit and drain fully ripe cherries. Put through food chopper. Measure 4½ cups and place in kettle. Add sugar and mix thoroughly. Place over high heat and bring to a rapid boil, stirring constantly. Boil until gel stage is reached. Stir in pectin and return to a full boil for 1 minute. Remove from heat, add almond extract and skim off foam. Pour hot mixture into hot sterilized glasses and seal immediately.

Strawberry Preserves
Makes about 4 eight-ounce jars

1 quart strawberries   **4 cups sugar**

Sort, wash, and hull strawberries. Put 1 cup water into large kettle and bring to a boil. Add sugar gradually, stirring until a heavy syrup is formed. Add strawberries and boil rapidly, uncovered, 9 minutes. Do not stir but shake kettle during boiling time. Ladle into flat pans or trays. Skim. Shake berries occasionally until they are cold. Pour mixture into hot sterilized jars and seal immediately.

Lemon-Strawberry Preserves
Makes about 6 eight-ounce jars

6 cups medium-ripe strawberries   **6 cups sugar**
  (about 1½ quarts)   **½ cup lemon juice**

Sort, wash and hull strawberries. Place in large kettle. Sprinkle sugar over top. Let stand, covered, at room temperature 3 to 4 hours until most of the sugar has turned to syrup. Place over moderately low heat and bring very slowly to a boil, stirring gently at intervals. Boil rapidly, uncovered, 10 minutes. Add lemon juice and cook 2 minutes longer. Syrup will be fairly thick but still quite runny. *Don't overcook*. Ladle into hot sterilized jars and seal immediately.

Cherry Preserves
Makes about 4 eight-ounce jars

1 quart pitted sour cherries   **4 cups sugar**
  (about 1¾ pounds)   **½ cup light corn syrup**

Place cherries in kettle and cover with sugar. Mix thoroughly. Stir in corn syrup. Bring mixture to a boil. Boil, uncovered, 15 minutes, shaking pan occasionally. Pour cherry mixture into flat pan or tray and let stand, covered, at room temperature 24 hours, stirring occasionally. Pour mixture into clean hot jars and seal immediately. Process 20 minutes in boiling-water bath.

Yellow Tomato Preserves
Makes about 4 eight-ounce jars

2 quarts small yellow tomatoes (about 3 pounds)
3 cups sugar
1 teaspoon salt

1 lemon, thinly sliced and seeded
¼ cup thinly sliced candied ginger

Wash and dry tomatoes. Cut a thin slice from the blossom end and press out seeds, being careful to keep tomatoes whole. Combine tomatoes, sugar and salt in a kettle. Simmer slowly until sugar is dissolved. Bring slowly to a boil, stirring constantly. Boil gently, uncovered, 40 minutes until syrup thickens. Add lemon slices and ginger. Continue boiling 10 minutes, stirring often. Remove from heat. Ladle into hot sterilized jars and seal immediately.

Caramel Peach Preserves
Makes 6 to 7 eight-ounce jars

8 cups peeled, sliced peaches (about 6 pounds)
3 peach pits

⅓ cup orange juice
1 pound light brown sugar
4 cups white sugar

Blanch, peel and slice medium-ripe peaches and measure. Place peaches, pits and orange juice in large kettle. Cover and cook over low heat 10 minutes. Add brown sugar and white sugar. Bring slowly to a boil, stirring constantly. Cook over moderate heat, stirring frequently, until syrup thickens and peaches are translucent. Remove from heat and discard peach pits. Ladle into hot sterilized jars and seal immediately.

Strawberry Conserve

Makes about 8 eight-ounce glasses

3 pints strawberries
2 cups chopped fresh pineapple
 (1 small to medium pineapple)
2 tablespoons lemon juice

1 cup seedless raisins
1 orange
8 cups sugar

Sort, wash, and hull berries. Crush slightly. Peel, core, and remove eyes from pineapple. Put through food chopper, using fine blade. Add lemon juice to pineapple. Put raisins through food chopper. Cut orange in sections, remove seeds, and put through food chopper. Combine all fruit and measure 8 cups crushed fruit. Add sugar and place in a large kettle. Cook mixture, uncovered, over moderate heat, until very thick, stirring very frequently. Pour hot mixture into hot sterilized glasses and seal immediately.

Grape Conserve

Makes about 7 eight-ounce glasses

4 cups halved, seeded purple
 grapes (about 1¾ pounds)
4 cups halved, seedless green
 grapes (about 1¾ pounds)

1 large lemon, thinly sliced
 and seeded
6 cups sugar
1 cup coarsely chopped walnuts
 (about ¼ pound shelled)

Combine grapes, lemon and ½ cup water in a large kettle. Bring slowly to a boil, reduce heat and simmer, covered, 20 minutes. Add sugar and stir over moderate heat until dissolved. Boil rapidly until gel stage is reached. Stir in walnuts. Remove from heat and skim off foam. Ladle hot mixture into hot sterilized glasses and seal immediately.

Cranberry-Brazil Nut Conserve
Makes about 6 eight-ounce glasses

4 cups cranberries (1 pound)
2½ cups sugar
1 cup seedless raisins
⅓ cup orange juice

Grated rind of 1 large lemon
1 cup chopped Brazil nuts
 (about ⅓ pound shelled)

Combine cranberries and 1 cup water in a large saucepan. Boil gently, uncovered, until soft. Press through a sieve or food mill, discarding skin and seeds. Return to saucepan. Add sugar, raisins, orange juice and grated lemon rind. Simmer mixture over low heat, stirring frequently, about 15 minutes. Stir in nuts and remove from heat. Ladle into hot sterilized glasses and seal immediately.

Damson Plum Conserve
Makes about 8 eight-ounce glasses

3 pounds Damson plums,
 chopped
1 orange, peeled and sliced
1 lemon, peeled and sliced

3 cups sugar
1 pound seedless raisins
1 cup coarsely chopped pecans
 (about ¼ pound shelled)

Combine plums, orange and lemon slices and ½ cup water in large kettle. Bring slowly to a boil. Reduce heat and simmer, covered, 20 minutes. Add sugar and raisins. Stir over moderate heat until sugar dissolves. Boil rapidly, uncovered, until gel stage is reached. Stir in pecans. Remove from heat and skim off foam. Ladle into hot sterilized glasses and seal immediately.

Peach-Grapefruit Conserve
Makes 7 to 8 eight-ounce glasses

8 cups diced peaches
(about 6 pounds)
3 medium grapefruit
Grated rind of 1 orange

6 cups sugar
1 tablespoon lemon juice
1 cup chopped blanched almonds
(about ¼ pound shelled)

Peel and dice enough fresh peaches to make 8 cups prepared fruit. Peel and section grapefruit. Cut sections into
small pieces the same size as the peaches. Put fruit into
large kettle. Add orange rind, sugar and lemon juice.
Bring to a boil and boil, stirring frequently, until mixture
is thick. Stir in almonds. Ladle into hot sterilized glasses
and seal immediately.

Tomato-Apple Conserve
Makes about 8 eight-ounce glasses

2 lemons, thinly sliced
and seeded
6 pounds ripe tomatoes
3 pounds tart apples
5 cups sugar
1 cup seedless raisins

½ teaspoon salt
¼ cup chopped candied or
preserved ginger
1 cup roughly chopped walnuts
(about ¼ pound shelled)

Place lemon slices in small saucepan and cover with cold
water. Bring to a boil and simmer until rind is very tender.
Drain off liquid and measure out 1 cup. Place lemon rind
and 1 cup liquid in large kettle. Peel tomatoes and cut in
large pieces. Add to kettle. Wash, peel and core apples.
Cut into ¾-inch cubes and put in kettle. Add sugar, raisins
and salt. Cook and stir over moderate heat until sugar
dissolves. Simmer, stirring often, until mixture thickens
and fruit is translucent. Stir in ginger and walnuts. Remove
from heat and ladle into hot sterilized glasses and seal
immediately.

GENERAL PROCEDURE
FOR MAKING MARMALADES

Wash and slice fruit very thin. Remove seeds. Measure fruit and for each cup of fruit add 1½ cups water. Cover and set aside overnight. Next morning measure fruit and liquid. For each cup measure ¾ cup sugar and set aside. Place fruit and liquid in kettle and boil, uncovered, 20 minutes. Add sugar and stir to dissolve. Boil, uncovered, until gel stage is reached. Remove from heat and allow to cool slightly. Stir to distribute fruit. Pour into hot sterilized glasses and seal immediately.

Suggested fruit combinations for marmalades
2 oranges and 1 lemon
4 grapefruit, 1 lemon, 1 bitter orange
4 bitter oranges, 8 sweet oranges, 2 lemons
1 grapefruit, 1 orange, 1 lemon
4 limes and 2 lemons
2 pineapples and 3 lemons

Note: *The best oranges to use for marmalade are bitter Seville oranges which until recently were grown only in Spain. Although they are readily available in most Canadian supermarkets, it is often difficult to obtain them in the United States. However, Florida has begun to grow Seville oranges and therefore, if neither you nor your grocer can locate them, contact the Florida Department of Agriculture and Conservation Service Division of Fruit and Vegetable Inspection, P.O. Box 1072, Winterhaven, Florida 33880. They will tell you where these oranges can be purchased.*

Scotch Marmalade
Makes about 20 pints

8 pounds Seville oranges	18 pounds sugar
4 lemons	

Grate the rinds from oranges and lemons. Set aside. Squeeze juice from fruit. Strain juice into large kettle. Place seeds and pulp in cheesecloth and tie loosely. Add rinds, cheesecloth bag and 12 quarts (48 cups) of water to juice in kettle. Bring to a boil and boil gently, uncovered, 2 to 3 hours or until liquid is reduced by one-third. Remove cheesecloth and squeeze juice out gently. Add sugar and stir until sugar is dissolved. Bring to a boil and boil vigorously, stirring frequently, 30 minutes. Continue boiling until mixture is thick and reaches the gel stage. Remove from heat and skim off foam. Let stand 10 minutes. Ladle into hot sterilized jars and seal immediately.

Tomato Marmalade
Makes 8 to 9 eight-ounce glasses

3 oranges	1 teaspoon salt
2 lemons	6 cinnamon sticks
3 quarts peeled, sliced	1 tablespoon whole cloves
ripe tomatoes	6 whole allspice
6 cups sugar	

Remove rind from oranges and lemons with a vegetable peeler. Cut into thin strips. Place in saucepan, cover with cold water and bring to a boil. Drain, cover with cold water, bring to a boil and simmer, covered, 15 minutes or until tender. Drain and reserve rind. Remove white membranes from oranges and lemons. Cut into small pieces, removing seeds. Place in large kettle with drained rind, tomatoes, sugar and salt. Tie spices in cheesecloth and add to tomato mixture. Bring slowly to a boil, stirring to dissolve sugar. Boil gently, stirring almost constantly, 1 hour or until marmalade is thick and reaches gel stage. Remove from heat and discard spice bag. Ladle mixture into hot sterilized glasses. Seal immediately.

Rhubarb Marmalade

Makes 3 to 4 eight-ounce glasses

3 cups diced rhubarb
(about 1 pound)
2 cups strawberries
(about ⅔ pound)

Juice and grated rind of 1 orange
2½ cups sugar

Wash, trim and dice rhubarb. Sort, wash and hull strawberries. Combine with orange juice and rind. Place in kettle, cover and allow to stand 1 hour in a cool place. Add sugar, mix well and bring to a boil over high heat. Boil, stirring frequently, until gel stage is reached. Remove from heat and skim off foam. Pour hot mixture into hot sterilized glasses and seal immediately.

Pineapple Marmalade

Makes 3 to 4 eight-ounce glasses

1 pineapple
3 cups sugar

Juice and grated rind
of 3 lemons

Peel and core pineapple, remove eyes, and cut in small pieces. Place pineapple, sugar, lemon juice and rind in kettle. Bring to a boil, reduce heat and simmer. Stir frequently until thick and gel stage is reached. Remove from heat and skim off foam. Pour hot mixture into hot sterilized glasses and seal immediately.

Apple Marmalade

Makes about 6 eight-ounce glasses

8 cups thinly sliced tart apples
(about 3 pounds)
1 orange

5 cups sugar
2 tablespoons lemon juice

Wash, pare, quarter and core apples. Cut into thin slices. Wash orange, remove seeds and thinly slice. Place sugar in kettle with 1½ cups water and heat until dissolved, add lemon juice and bring to a boil. Add apples and orange slices. Boil over high heat, stirring constantly, until mixture thickens and gel stage is reached. Remove from heat and skim off foam. Pour hot mixture into hot sterilized glasses and seal immediately.

Pear-Ginger Marmalade

Makes about 5 eight-ounce glasses

1 lemon	3 cups sugar
1 orange	1 ounce preserved ginger,
2 pounds pears	cut into very thin strips

Squeeze juice from lemon and orange. Reserve juice, discard pulp, and cut peel into very thin strips. Place peel in saucepan with 1 cup water and simmer, covered, 20 minutes. Drain and finely chop. Wash, peel and core pears. Cut into small pieces. Place pears, citrus juice and peel in large kettle and simmer until tender, about 10 minutes. Add sugar and ginger. Bring to a boil. Stir to dissolve sugar. Boil, stirring constantly, until thick and clear, and gel stage is reached. Remove from heat and skim off foam. Pour hot mixture into hot sterilized glasses and seal immediately.

Peach-Orange Marmalade

Makes about 6 eight-ounce glasses

5 cups finely chopped peaches (about 4 pounds)	2 tablespoons lemon juice
	6 cups sugar
1 cup finely chopped orange (about 2 oranges)	2 cups chopped maraschino cherries (optional)
Rind of 1 additional orange, shredded	

Sort, wash, peel and pit peaches. Wash 2 oranges, peel and remove seeds. Put peaches and orange pulp through a food chopper using coarse blade. Shred rind from all 3 oranges. Measure 5 cups peaches and 1 cup orange pulp. Place in kettle with all ingredients except cherries. Mix thoroughly. Bring to a boil and boil over high heat, stirring constantly, until mixture thickens and gel stage is reached. Add maraschino cherries if desired. Remove from heat and skim off foam. Pour hot mixture into hot sterilized glasses and seal immediately.

Kumquat Marmalade
Makes about 8 eight-ounce glasses

24 kumquats	Sugar (about 9 cups)
2 oranges	Juice of 2 lemons

Sort and wash kumquats and slice very thin. Wash and seed oranges. Chop pulp and rind. Combine fruit and measure. Place in kettle with 3 cups water for each cup of fruit. Let stand in cool place 12 hours or overnight. Bring to a full boil, cover, reduce heat and simmer until rind is tender. Measure cooked fruit. Add 1 cup sugar for each cup fruit. Stir in lemon juice. Return to boil and boil, stirring occasionally, until gel stage is reached. Remove from heat and skim off foam. Pour hot mixture into hot sterilized glasses and seal immediately.

Lime Marmalade
Makes 7 to 8 eight-ounce glasses

4 cups sliced limes (10 to 12 medium)	Sugar

Slice limes into very thin slices, discarding end pieces. Cut slices into quarters. Measure. Place limes in an enamel kettle. Cover with 6 cups cold water and let stand, covered, 12 to 18 hours at room temperature. Place over moderate heat and cook, covered, 20 to 25 minutes or until lime peel is very tender. Remove from heat and measure cooked mixture. For each cup of cooked lime, add 1 cup sugar. Return mixture to kettle. Stir over moderate heat until sugar dissolves. Boil rapidly, stirring frequently, until marmalade reaches gel stage. Remove from heat and skim. Ladle into hot sterilized glasses and seal immediately.

Amber Marmalade
Makes about 6 eight-ounce glasses

1 grapefruit	1 lemon
2 oranges	Sugar (about 7 cups)

Wash fruit and slice very thin, discarding end pieces and seeds. Quarter grapefruit slices, cut orange and lemon slices in half. Measure fruit and place in kettle. Add 1 cup water for each cup fruit. Cover and let stand in a cool place 12 hours or overnight. Bring to a boil and boil, stirring frequently, until peel is tender. Measure fruit and cooking liquid. Add 1 cup sugar for each cup combined cooked fruit and liquid. Stir to dissolve sugar. Return to boil and boil, stirring frequently, until gel stage is reached. Pour hot mixture into hot sterilized glasses and seal immediately.

Apple Butter
Makes 7 to 8 eight-ounce glasses

4 pounds tart cooking apples	3 teaspoons ground cinnamon
2 cups cider or water	1½ teaspoons ground cloves
Sugar	½ teaspoon allspice

Wash apples and cut in quarters. Do not peel or remove cores. Place in kettle, cover and boil gently in cider or water until very soft. Put through a sieve or food mill, discarding seeds and skins. Measure pulp and for each cup of pulp add ½ cup sugar. Return to kettle and stir in spices. Simmer, stirring constantly, until mixture is very thick and reaches the gel stage. Remove from heat, pour into hot sterilized glasses and seal immediately.

Apricot Butter

Makes about 5 eight-ounce glasses

2½ pounds fresh apricots
1 cup orange juice
Sugar

¾ teaspoon nutmeg
1 teaspoon ground cinnamon

Wash, pit and mash apricots. Combine pulp with orange juice in a kettle. Cook, covered, until pulp is tender. Put the pulp through a food mill, discarding skins. Measure purée. For each cup of purée add ¾ cup sugar. Blend in spices. Boil gently over moderate heat, stirring constantly, until thick. Remove from heat and pour into hot sterilized glasses. Seal immediately.

Port Apple Butter

Makes about 6 eight-ounce glasses

1 bottle (⅘ quart) port wine
8 large Golden Delicious apples
1½ cups sugar

¼ teaspoon salt
½ teaspoon ground cinnamon
1 whole cinnamon stick

Combine port and 4 cups water in a large kettle. Bring to a boil over high heat. Peel and thinly slice apples. There should be about 8 cups. Add apples to wine mixture and simmer, uncovered, stirring occasionally, for 45 minutes. Stir in sugar, salt and cinnamon. Cook over medium heat, stirring often, until mixture is as thick as hot applesauce, about 20 to 25 minutes. Remove from heat, discard cinnamon stick, and pour into hot sterilized glasses. Seal immediately.

October Butter

Makes about 5 eight-ounce glasses

8 medium cooking apples
2 large firm Anjou pears
3 cups orange juice
2 cinnamon sticks

2 cups mashed ripe banana
(about 3 to 4 medium bananas)
2 tablespoons lemon juice
Sugar

Wash apples and pears. Cut into small pieces, but do not peel or remove cores. Place in a large kettle with orange juice and cinnamon sticks. Cover and cook over moderate heat until very soft, about 45 minutes to 1 hour. Remove cinnamon sticks. Force cooked mixture through a food mill, discarding skins and seeds. Combine apple-pear mixture with mashed banana and lemon juice in a kettle. Boil gently until mixture is thick enough to mound slightly on a spoon. Stir frequently during cooking. Measure thickened fruit mixture and return to kettle. Add half as much sugar as there was measured fruit mixture (e.g., 3 cups of sugar for 6 cups of fruit pulp). Boil gently, stirring frequently, until thickened, about 20 to 25 minutes. Remove from heat and pour into hot sterilized glasses. Seal immediately.

Tomato Butter

Makes about 4 eight-ounce glasses

4 pounds ripe tomatoes
2½ cups firmly packed
 light brown sugar
1½ teaspoons cinnamon

1¼ teaspoons ground cloves
¼ teaspoon allspice
Pinch of salt

Blanch, peel and cut tomatoes in quarters. Place in a large kettle and simmer, covered, stirring occasionally, until soft and mushy. Measure tomatoes. There should be about 6 cups. Put back into kettle with remaining ingredients. Bring to a boil, lower heat and simmer, uncovered, stirring frequently, until thick, about 45 minutes. Remove from heat and pour into hot sterilized glasses. Seal immediately.

6 JELLY

Jellies are made by cooking fruit then extracting the juice by placing cooked fruit in a jelly bag and allowing juice to drip through into a bowl. The extracted juice is tested for pectin content and boiled with sugar until the gel stage is reached. It is then poured hot into hot sterilized jelly glasses and sealed.

> **IMPORTANT:** *Read about Acid, Sugar, Pectin, Pectin and Acid Content of Fruit, Jelly Glasses, Sealing and Paraffin Wax in Jams, Preserves, Conserves, Marmalades and Butters, pages 57-61.*

FRUIT FOR JELLY

The type of fruit to be used is a major consideration in making jelly. Fruit, or combinations of fruit, with good pectin and acid content must be used unless commercial pectin is to be added. Jellies that are particularly simple to make include currant, sour apple, gooseberry, plum, grape, crabapple, cranberry and quince.

COOKING FRUIT

Fruit should be washed thoroughly. Berries may be crushed slightly to release some of the juice.

Do not peel, core, or remove the seeds from fruit unless recipe directs. Berries, such as currants, contain a substantial amount of juice, and therefore they require the addition of only a small amount of water before cooking. Apples, quinces and crabapples do not contain quite as much juice as berries, and therefore require a little more water in order to extract the juice. In all cases, add only enough water to prevent fruit from burning. Excess water will dilute natural pectin.

Cooking time for fruit will vary. Juicy fruit may require as little as five or 10 minutes to release the juice, while firmer fruit may require as long as 30 minutes.

EXTRACTING JUICE IN A JELLY BAG

A damp jelly bag, or several layers of damp cheesecloth, may be used to extract juice. Suspend the jelly bag over a large bowl or line a colander with cheesecloth and place the colander in a large bowl, allow the corners of the cheesecloth to extend well over the sides of the colander. Pour fruit and juice into the cloth and tie the four corners together. Allow the juice to drip into the bowl. It may take several hours to extract all the juice. Resist the temptation to hurry the process by squeezing the bag since this will result in cloudy jelly.

PREPARING JARS

While the fruit juice is draining, prepare jars or jelly glasses. Check for flaws and wash in hot suds. Then sterilize 20 minutes in boiling water. Lids should be boiled five minutes. Leave jars and lids in hot water until needed.

TESTING FOR PECTIN CONTENT

Extracted juice should be tested for pectin by mixing 1 tablespoon of fruit juice with 1 tablespoon of grain alcohol (nonpoisonous denatured). Juice with a high pectin content will form a bulky clot, a medium pectin content will form two to three smaller clots, and a poor pectin content will form several small clots. (See illustration page 58.) When pectin content is not high, the juice must be boiled to make a concentrate by evaporating excess water, or commercial pectin must be added in order to obtain a good gel. Be certain to follow package instructions when using commercial pectin.

COOKING JELLY

Jelly should be made in small batches, usually not more than 8 cups of juice at a time. Measure juice, bring to a boil, and stir in sugar until dissolved. Bring to a boil again and boil rapidly, uncovered, until gel stage is reached.

A large, heavy kettle should be used to boil juice and sugar, uncovered. This will allow juice to boil rapidly without boiling over. A wide kettle will allow good evaporation and the gel stage will be reached more quickly.

GEL STAGE

Sheeting Test

The usual way of determining when jelly point has been reached is to use the "sheeting" test. Dip up some of the boiling jelly with a metal spoon, then let it pour off the spoon back into the kettle. Jelly point is reached when the last two drops on the spoon cling together, form a sheet, and are very slow dropping off; or when they cling to the edge of the spoon in a sheet; or when drops run together. Carefully remove scum and pour jelly into hot, sterilized glasses.

Temperature Test

Although many people like to use a thermometer when making jelly, there is no really accurate test we know of to indicate exact gel stage by temperature. However, when the thermometer reading is around 220°F, gel stage (for all sugar jellies) is close. For best results use the sheeting test or calculate 8°F above boiling water temperature in your area.

FILLING JARS

Remove jars or glasses from water as needed, one at a time. Fill jar to within ½ inch of top. Seal immediately if using metal lid and screw band. Allow the jelly to cool slightly before sealing with paraffin.

GENERAL PROCEDURE FOR MAKING JELLY

1. Read recipe through and make sure all ingredients and necessary equipment are on hand.
2. Select fruit. Use approximately half ripe fruit and half underripe fruit. *Never use overripe fruit.*
3. Wash fruit thoroughly and cut away bruised or damaged spots.
4. Prepare and cook fruit as recipe directs.
5. Pour the hot fruit into a moistened jelly bag or several thicknesses of cheesecloth.
6. Hang jelly bag over bowl to drip. Don't squeeze bag; it will make jelly cloudy.
7. Prepare jelly glasses. Check for nicks, chips and scratches. Wash in hot suds. Sterilize 20 minutes in boiling water. Boil lids five minutes. Allow jars and lids to remain in water until needed.
8. Measure extracted juice. (Approximately 8 cups of juice is the most satisfactory amount to work with for each batch of jelly.)
9. Bring juice to a boil and test for pectin.
10. Add sugar and stir to dissolve.
11. Bring to a boil and boil rapidly about 10 minutes or until the gel stage is reached.

12. Remove from heat. Skim off foam.
13. Pour into hot sterilized jelly glasses.
14. Cool slightly and seal with paraffin or seal immediately if using metal lids.
15. Cap with protective metal cover.
16. Label, indicating contents and date.
17. Store in cool, dry place.

JELLY TABLE

The juices, or combination of juices, suggested are particularly good for making jelly. In the first column, where combinations of juices are shown, the fractions indicate the recommended proportion of one juice to another.

Fruit Juices and Combinations	Amount of Sugar to One Cup Juice
Apple	⅔ to ¾ cup
Blueberry, Blackberry, or Loganberry	¾ to 1 cup
Crabapple	⅔ to ¾ cup
Cranberry	1 cup
Currant	¾ to 1 cup
Gooseberry	¾ cup
Grape	¾ to 1 cup
Blackberry ¼, Apple ¾	⅔ cup
Black Raspberry ½, Apple ½	⅔ cup
Black Raspberry ⅔, Currant ⅓	¾ cup
Cherry ½, Apple ½	⅔ cup
Elderberry ½, Apple ½	¾ to 1 cup
Gooseberry ¾, Currant ¼	1 cup
Peach ½, Apple ½	⅔ cup
Plum ¼, Crabapple ¾	1 cup
Quince ⅓, Cranberry ⅓, Apple ⅓	¾ cup
Quince ½, Apple ½	⅔ cup
Red Raspberry ⅓, Currant ⅔	1 cup
Rhubarb ½, Apple ½	⅔ cup

Grape Jelly
Makes 8 to 9 eight-ounce glasses

4 cups grape juice (about 3½
  pounds fully ripe Concord
  grapes plus ½ cup water)

7 cups sugar
½ bottle (3 ounces) liquid pectin

Sort and wash grapes. Remove stems. Crush grapes, add ½ cup water. Place in large kettle, cover, bring to a boil over high heat. Reduce heat and simmer 10 minutes. Remove from heat and extract juice. Allow juice to stand in a cool place overnight to prevent formation of tartrate crystals in jelly. Strain through double thickness of damp cheesecloth. Measure 4 cups of juice into kettle. Stir in sugar. Quickly bring to a full rolling boil, stirring constantly. Add pectin. Return to full boil and boil hard 1 minute. Remove from heat and skim off foam. Pour hot jelly into hot sterilized jelly glasses and seal immediately.

Apple Jelly
Makes 3 to 4 eight-ounce glasses

4 cups apple juice (about 3
  pounds tart apples plus 3
  cups water)

2 tablespoons lemon juice
  (optional)
3 cups sugar

Use ¼ underripe apples and ¾ fully ripe, firm, tart apples. Wash thoroughly, remove stems and blossoms. Do not pare or core. Cut into small pieces and place in large kettle. Add 3 cups water, cover, bring to a boil over high heat. Reduce heat and simmer until soft, about 20 to 25 minutes. Extract juice. Measure 4 cups of juice into kettle. Add lemon juice and sugar and mix thoroughly. Bring to a boil and boil over high heat until gel stage is reached. Remove from heat and skim off foam. Pour hot jelly into hot sterilized jelly glasses and seal immediately.

Mint-Apple Jelly

Makes 3 to 4 eight-ounce glasses

1 cup firmly packed mint leaves

**1 recipe Apple Jelly (above)
Green food colouring**

Wash mint, remove leaves from stems, sort and measure. Place in bowl and cover with 1 cup boiling water. Allow to stand one hour. Press juice from leaves and measure. Prepare recipe for Apple Jelly above, adding 8 tablespoons mint juice to extracted apple juice. Tint jelly with a few drops of green food colouring just before filling jelly glasses.

Orange Jelly

Makes about 4 eight-ounce glasses

**1 can (6 ounces) frozen undiluted orange juice concentrate
3 tablespoons lemon juice**

**1 tablespoon grated orange rind
3½ cups sugar
½ bottle (3 ounces) liquid pectin**

Combine orange juice, lemon juice, orange rind and 1¼ cups water in a large saucepan. Add sugar. Stir over moderate heat until sugar dissolves and mixture comes to a boil. Stir in pectin all at once. Stir continuously and bring to a full rolling boil. Boil hard 1 minute. Remove from heat and skim off foam. Pour hot mixture into hot sterilized glasses and seal immediately.

Orange-Sauternes Jelly

Makes 4 to 6 eight-ounce glasses

**1 teaspoon finely grated orange rind
1½ cups Sauternes or other sweet white wine
½ cup orange juice**

**2 tablespoons lemon juice
4 cups sugar or
  4 cups mild honey
½ bottle (3 ounces) liquid pectin**

Combine orange rind, wine, orange and lemon juice in kettle. Bring mixture to a full boil. Stir in sugar or honey. Reduce heat and simmer, uncovered, 3 minutes. Stir in pectin, return to full boil and boil hard 1 minute. Remove from heat and skim off foam. Pour hot jelly into hot sterilized glasses and seal immediately.

Currant Jelly (Bar-le-Duc)

Makes about 4 eight-ounce glasses

4 cups currant juice
(about 2½ quarts currants,
plus 1 cup water)

4 cups sugar

Use ¼ underripe and ¾ fully ripe currants. Sort and wash currants but do not remove stems. Drain and place in large kettle. Crush berries, add 1 cup water, cover and bring to a boil. Reduce heat and simmer, covered, 10 minutes. Extract juice. Measure 4 cups of juice into kettle. Bring to a rapid boil, add sugar and stir to dissolve. Continue to boil until gel stage is reached. Remove from heat and skim off foam. Pour hot jelly into hot sterilized jelly glasses and seal immediately.

Rose Hip Jelly

Makes 4 to 6 eight-ounce glasses

2 cups rose hip juice
(about 1 pound rose hips
plus 1 cup water)
3 cups apple juice
(about 2 pounds apples
plus 2 cups water)

5 tablespoons lemon juice
(optional)
3¾ cups sugar
Red and yellow food colouring

Wash and stem rose hips. Place in kettle, cover with 1 cup water, bring to a boil. Reduce heat and simmer, covered, until soft. Use ¼ underripe apples and ¾ ripe, firm, tart apples. Wash thoroughly, remove stems and blossoms. Do not peel or core. Cut into small pieces and place in separate kettle. Cover with 2 cups water, bring to a boil. Reduce heat and simmer, covered, until soft. Extract juice from both fruits. Combine 2 cups rose hip juice with 3 cups apple juice in a kettle. Add lemon juice and sugar. Mix thoroughly. Bring to a boil and boil over high heat until gel stage is reached. Remove from heat and skim off foam. Tint with a few drops of food colouring. Pour hot jelly into hot sterilized glasses and seal immediately.

Note: *Rose hips, available after the first frost, should never be used if roses have been sprayed with insecticide.*

Rhubarb-Strawberry Jelly
Makes about 3 eight-ounce glasses

6 cups sliced unpeeled rhubarb
  (about 3 pounds)
1 pint strawberries, washed,
  hulled and puréed

3¼ cups sugar
1 bottle (6 ounces) liquid pectin

Wash and slice rhubarb. Place in a saucepan with 1 cup water. Bring to a boil. Reduce heat and simmer, covered, 10 to 15 minutes or until rhubarb is very soft and comes apart in strings. Remove from heat and stir in puréed strawberries. Extract juice. There should be 2 cups of juice. If there is less, add water to make 2 cups. Combine juice and sugar in a large saucepan. Stir over moderate heat until sugar dissolves and mixture comes to a boil. Stir in liquid pectin all at once and continue to stir. Bring to a full rolling boil and boil hard 1 minute. Remove from heat and skim off foam. Pour hot mixture into hot sterilized glasses and seal immediately.

Champagne Jelly
Makes 4 eight-ounce glasses

1 package (1¾ ounces)
  powdered pectin

3 cups champagne
4 cups sugar

Combine pectin with ¾ cup water in large saucepan. Bring to a rapid boil over high heat, stirring constantly. Boil hard 1 minute. Reduce heat. Add champagne and sugar. Simmer about 5 minutes until sugar is dissolved, stirring constantly. Remove from heat and skim off foam. Pour hot jelly into hot sterilized jelly glasses and seal immediately.

7 PICKLES, RELISHES, CHUTNEY AND SAUCES

Pickles, relishes and chutney all have a special role at mealtime. They add colour, flavour, texture and a special tang of their own to almost every meal. The sweet, sour and salty flavour of pickled fruit and vegetables is easy to achieve, and in general the pickling process is quite simple. Beginners may find this a good place to start to familiarize themselves with equipment and methods of preserving.

Pickling is divided into four different categories, each based on the method of preparation and ingredients used.

Brined pickles, also called fermented pickles, go through a curing process of about three weeks. Dilled cucumbers and sauerkraut belong to this group. Other vegetables, such as green tomatoes, may also be cured in the same way. Curing changes cucumber colour from bright green to olive or yellow green. The white interior of the fresh cucumber becomes uniformly translucent. A fine flavour, neither too salty, sour, nor spicy, develops during curing. Cucumber dills may be flavoured with garlic, if desired. The skin of the pickle should be tender and firm, but not hard, rubbery or shriveled. The inside should be tender and firm, but not softy or mushy.

Fresh-pack or quick-process pickles, such as crosscut cucumber slices, whole cucumber dills, sweet gherkins, and dilled green beans, are brined several hours or overnight, drained and combined with boiling hot vinegar, spices, and other seasonings. They are quick and easy to prepare and have a tart, pungent flavour. Seasonings may be selected to suit individual preferences. Fresh-pack whole cucumbers should be olive green, crisp, tender yet firm.

Fruit pickles are usually prepared from whole fruit and simmered in a spicy, sweet-sour syrup. They should be a bright colour, of uniform size, and tender yet firm without being watery. Pears, peaches and watermelon rind are prepared this way.

Relishes are made from fruit and vegetables which are chopped, seasoned, and cooked to a desired consistency. Clear, bright colour and uniformity in size of pieces will make an attractive relish. They serve as an accent to the flavour of other food.

INGREDIENTS FOR SUCCESSFUL PICKLING

Satisfactory pickles result when good quality ingredients are used and proper procedures are followed. Correct proportions of fruit or vegetable, sugar, salt, vinegar and spices are essential. Alum and lime are not needed to make pickles crisp and firm if good quality ingredients are used and up-to-date procedures are followed.

Use tested recipes. Read the complete recipe before starting. Make certain necessary ingredients are on hand. Measure or weigh all ingredients carefully.

Fruit and Vegetables

Select tender vegetables and firm fruit. Choose one of the many varieties of cucumber especially developed for pickling; eating cucumbers do not make the best pickles. Use unwaxed cucumbers for pickling whole. Brine cannot penetrate waxed cucumbers. Pears and peaches may be slightly underripe for pickling. Sort produce for uniform size and select the size best suited for the recipe. Use fruit and vegetables as soon as possible after picking or purchasing. If the fruit and vegetables cannot be used immediately, refrigerate or store where they will be well ventilated and kept cool. This is particularly important for cucumbers because they deteriorate rapidly at room temperature. Never use fruit or vegetables that show even slight evidence of mould.

To prepare, wash fruit and vegetables thoroughly in cold water, whether they are to be pared or not. Use a brush and wash only a few at a time under running water or through several changes of water. Clinging soil may contain bacteria that are hard to destroy. Lift fruit or vegetables out of the water, so soil that has been washed off will not be drained back over them. Rinse pan thoroughly between washings. Handle gently to avoid bruising. Be sure to remove all stem ends from cucumbers. They may be a source of the enzymes responsible for the softening of cucumbers during fermentation.

Salt

Use coarse salt. Iodized salt will make pickles dark and salt with anti-caking additives will cloud pickling brines.

Vinegar

Use a good quality vinegar. Cider vinegar, with its mellow, acid taste, gives a nice blending of flavours, but it may darken white or light-coloured fruit and vegetables. White distilled vinegar has a sharp, pungent, acetic acid taste and is desirable when light colour is important, as it is for pickled pears, onions and cauliflower. Do not dilute vinegar unless the recipe specifies. If a less sour pickle is preferred, add sugar instead of decreasing the vinegar.

Sugar

Either white granulated sugar or brown sugar may be used. White sugar is preferable, unless brown sugar is called for in the recipe. Brown sugar may darken food slightly.

Spices

Spices include both sweet herbs and pungent spices. Herbs are the dried leaves of aromatic plants grown in the temperate zone. Spices are the dried stems, leaves, roots, seeds, flowers, buds and bark of aromatic plants grown in the tropics. Fresh spices always provide the best flavour. They deteriorate rapidly and lose their pungency in heat and humidity. If they cannot be used immediately, they should be stored in airtight containers in a cool place.

EQUIPMENT

Use unchipped enamelware, stainless steel, aluminum or glass for heating pickling liquids. Do not use copper, brass, galvanized or iron utensils. These metals may react with acids or salts and cause undesirable colour changes in pickles or form undesirable compounds.

Use a crock or stone jar, an unchipped enamel-lined pan, or a large glass jar, bowl or casserole for fermenting or brining. A heavy plate or large glass lid is necessary to fit inside container to cover vegetables in the brine. Use a weight, such as a glass jar filled with water, to hold cover down and keep vegetables below surface of the brine.

Small utensils that are helpful include: measuring spoons, large wooden or stainless steel spoons for stirring, measuring cups, sharp knives, large trays, tongs, vegetable peelers, ladle with lip for pouring, slotted spoon, footed colander or wire basket, large-mouthed funnel, food chopper or grinder, and wooden cutting board.

Household scales will be needed if the recipes specify ingredients by weight.

Glass Jars and Lids

Select jars and lids that are free of cracks, chips, rust, dents or any defect that may prevent airtight seals and cause needless spoilage. Jars for pickles that will undergo processing in a water-bath processor need not be sterilized. Jars to be used for pickles, relishes, chutney or sauces that will not be processed after filling and sealing must be sterilized for 20 minutes in boiling water and removed one at a time as needed. Metal lids should be boiled five minutes and fitted and sealed with screw bands, one at a time as needed.

GENERAL PROCEDURE FOR PICKLING

1. Read through recipe to make sure all ingredients and equipment are on hand. Note that some pickle recipes are prepared in two or three stages, with several hours between each stage.
2. Fill water-bath ⅔ full, cover and begin heating.
3. Check jars for nicks, cracks and chips. Wash jars and lids in hot suds. Rinse well.
4. Wash vegetables thoroughly in cold water according to previous instructions.
5. Prepare recipe.
6. If recipe does *not* call for processing, sterilize jars 20 minutes in boiling water. Sterilize lids five minutes. When making unprocessed pickles, keep food boiling on top of stove and fill hot sterilized jars one at a time.
7. If recipe calls for processing, wash jars in hot soapy water, rinse well and leave in hot water until needed for filling. Sterilize lids five minutes and leave in water until needed for sealing.
8. Fill jar to ⅛ inch from sealing edge. Run a clean knife inside jar between food and jar to release air bubbles.
9. Use a clean paper towel or damp cloth to wipe sealing edge and threads of jar. Seal each jar immediately.
10. If recipe does *not* call for processing, place jars upright, well apart, on a wooden board or rubber mat and leave to cool. Don't set jars in a draft or on cold wet surfaces.
11. If recipe calls for processing, follow instructions for processing in water bath (14 and 15, page 41) or follow recipe instructions when given.
12. A popping noise may be heard with vacuum type lids. This indicates the seal has taken effect.
13. When cool, test for seal (page 35).
14. If seal has not taken effect, food may be reboiled within 24 hours, with a little extra vinegar to compensate for evaporation, and repacked into clean, hot,

sterilized jars, and sealed immediately with new lids. Care should be taken not to overcook pickles that are meant to be crisp.
15. Wipe jars with a wet cloth. Label, indicating contents and date.
16. Store in a cool, dark, dry place.

Note: *The United States Department of Agriculture recommends that pickles be processed in a boiling-water bath.*

Altitude Corrections
Processing times given in recipes are for altitudes less than 1,000 feet above sea level. At altitudes of 1,000 feet or above, increase the processing time according to the chart below:

Altitude (Feet)	Increase in processing time (minutes)
1,000	1
2,000	2
3,000	3
4,000	4
5,000	5
6,000	6
7,000	7
8,000	8
9,000	9
10,000	10

COMMON CAUSES OF POOR QUALITY PICKLES

Shriveled pickles may result from: too strong a vinegar, sugar, or salt solution at start of pickling process (for very sweet or very sour pickles start with a dilute solution and increase gradually to desired strength) overcooking or overprocessing.

Hollow pickles usually result from: poor quality cucumbers; overripe cucumbers; cucumbers processed more than 24 hours after picking; too rapid fermentation; too strong, or too weak, a brine during fermentation.

Soft or slippery pickles generally result from microbial action which causes spoilage. Once a pickle becomes soft it cannot be made firm. Microbial activity may be caused by: too little salt or acid; cucumbers not covered with brine during fermentation; scum scattered throughout brine during fermentation period; insufficient heat treatment; a seal that is not airtight; moldy garlic or spices.

Blossoms, if not entirely removed from the cucumbers before fermentation, may contain fungi or yeasts responsible for enzymatic softening of pickles.

Dark pickles may be caused by: use of ground spices; too much spice; iodized salt; overcooking; minerals, especially iron in water; use of iron utensils.

Brined Dill Pickles
Makes 9 to 10 quarts

20 pounds cucumbers, 3 to 6 inches long (about ½ bushel)
3 bunches fresh dill
¾ cup mixed pickling spice
10 cloves garlic, peeled, or to taste (optional)
2½ cups cider vinegar, (if light-coloured pickles are desired, substitute white vinegar)
1¾ cups coarse salt
2½ gallons water

Wash cucumbers thoroughly in cold water with a vegetable brush. Handle gently to avoid bruising. Remove all blossoms. Drain on rack or wipe dry. Place half of dill in a 5-gallon crock or jar. Fill crock with cucumbers to within 3 or 4 inches of top. Put pickling spice and dill over cucumbers. Add garlic if desired. Combine vinegar, salt and water. Mix throughly and pour over cucumbers. Cover with heavy china or glass plate, or with a lid that fits inside crock. Use a weight to hold plate down and to keep cucumbers under brine. (A glass jar filled with water makes an excellent weight.) Cover loosely with cloth.

Keep pickles at room temperature. Scum may start forming within 3 to 5 days. Remove scum daily. Do not stir pickles, but keep completely covered with brine. If necessary, make additional brine, using original proportions in recipe.

In about 3 weeks cucumbers will be an olive green colour and should have a good flavour. White spots inside fermented cucumbers will disappear during processing.

The original brine is usually cloudy as a result of yeast development during fermentation. If this cloudiness is objectionable, fresh brine may be made to cover pickles in jars. However, fermentation-brine is preferable because it has a desirable flavour. If used, strain before boiling.

Pack between 7 to 10 pickles into clean hot quart jars. Add some of the dill and 1 or 2 cloves of garlic per jar if desired. Do not pack tightly. Cover with *boiling* brine, leaving ½-inch headspace. Seal immediately.

Process on rack in boiling water 15 minutes. Processing procedure for fermented cucumbers and sauerkraut is slightly different from the usual water-bath procedure because processing time begins as soon as hot jars are placed in actively boiling water. This procedure prevents an undesirable cooked flavour and also prevents the loss of crispness important for good pickles.

Remove jars. Check seals. Set jars upright, several inches apart, on a wire rack to cool.

Sauerkraut
Makes 16 to 18 quarts

50 pounds cabbage   **2 cups coarse salt**

Remove outer leaves and any undesirable portions from firm mature heads of cabbage. Wash and drain. Cut into halves or quarters and remove core. Use a shredder or sharp knife to cut cabbage into thin shreds about the thickness of a dime. In a large container, thoroughly mix 3 tablespoons salt with 5 pounds shredded cabbage. Let the salted cabbage stand several minutes to wilt slightly. This will allow packing without excessive breaking or bruising of shreds.

Pack salted cabbage firmly and evenly into a large clean crock or jar. Use a wooden spoon or tamper, or your hands to press cabbage down firmly until juice comes to the surface. Repeat shredding, salting, and packing of cabbage until crock is filled to within 3 or 4 inches of top.

Cover cabbage with a clean, thin cloth (such as muslin) and tuck the edges down against the inside of the container so the cabbage is not exposed to air. Put a weight on top of the cover so the juice comes up to the cover but not over it. A water-filled jar makes a good weight.

Another way of covering cabbage during fermentation is to place a plastic bag, filled with water, on top of the fermenting cabbage. The water-filled bag seals the surface from exposure to air, and prevents the growth of film yeast or moulds. It also serves as a weight. For extra protection, the water-filled bag can be placed inside another plastic bag. Bags should be heavy, watertight plastic, safe for use with foods. The amount of water in the bag can be adjusted to give just enough pressure to keep fermenting cabbage covered with juice.

When fermentation begins remove scum daily and place a clean cloth over cabbage. Wash plate daily. Fermentation is usually completed in 5 to 6 weeks. Appearance, and taste will tell you when sauerkraut is fermented. The formation of gas bubbles indicates fermentation is taking place.

After fermentation, heat sauerkraut to simmering, but do not boil. Pack hot sauerkraut in clean, hot jars and cover with hot juice, leaving ½-inch headspace. Seal. Process in boiling-water bath, 15 minutes for pints, 20 minutes for quarts. Start to count processing time as soon as hot jars are placed in actively boiling water. Remove jars and set upright, several inches apart on wire rack to cool.

Spoilage in Sauerkraut

Spoilage in sauerkraut is indicated by undesirable colour, strange odour, odd flavour and soft texture.

Soft sauerkraut may result from: insufficient salt; too high a temperature during fermentation; uneven distribution of salt; air pockets caused by improper packing.

Pink sauerkraut is caused by growth of certain types of yeast on the surface, which grow as a result of: uneven distribution of salt; too much salt; improper covering or weighting during fermentation.

Dark sauerkraut may be caused by: unwashed and improperly trimmed cabbage; insufficient juice to cover fermenting cabbage; uneven distribution of salt; exposure to air; high temperatures during fermentation, processing or storage; over-long storage period.

Rotted sauerkraut is a condition usually found on the surface, where cabbage has not been covered sufficiently to exclude air during fermentation.

Mixed Sweet Pickles
Makes about 6 pints

2 medium heads cauliflower
2 sweet red peppers, seeded and cut into strips
2 green peppers, seeded and cut into strips
1 pound small white onions, cut in halves
4 cups white vinegar
2 cups sugar
½ cup light corn syrup
1 tablespoon mustard seed
1 tablespoon celery seed
1 teaspoon whole cloves
¼ teaspoon turmeric
2 tablespoons coarse salt

Wash and clean cauliflower and break into tiny flowerets. Measure 8 cups of cauliflower. Place in kettle, cover, and boil gently in a small amount of boiling salted water 5 minutes. Drain. Combine remaining ingredients in a large kettle. Bring to a boil. Add cauliflower and boil, uncovered, 2 minutes. Pack into clean hot pint jars, leaving ⅛-inch headspace. Seal immediately. Process 15 minutes in boiling-water bath.

Mustard Pickles
Makes about 5 quarts

2 quarts small pickling cucumbers
2 quarts tiny white onions
1 large cauliflower
4 sweet red peppers
1 cup coarse salt

1 cup all-purpose flour
6 tablespoons dry mustard
1½ cups sugar
1 tablespoon turmeric
8 cups cider vinegar

Wash cucumbers and cut into slices or chunks. Do not peel. Wash and peel onions. Wash cauliflower and break into small flowerets. Wash peppers, remove seeds, and chop coarsely. Combine vegetables in a large bowl. Combine salt and 2 cups water and pour over vegetables. Cover and let stand overnight at room temperature. In the morning bring vegetables and brine just to boiling point, but do not boil. Drain thoroughly. Combine flour, mustard, sugar and turmeric in a kettle. Add just enough cold vinegar to make paste. Stir in remaining vinegar. Bring to a boil, stirring, and boil until thick and creamy. Add well-drained vegetables and simmer just until vegetables are tender but not overcooked. Pack into clean hot quart jars, leaving ⅛-inch headspace. Seal immediately. Process 10 minutes in boiling-water bath.

Bread and Butter Pickles
Makes about 6 pints

25 cucumbers, 1 to 1½ inches
   in diameter
8 large onions
½ cup coarse salt
5 cups cider vinegar

5 cups sugar
2 tablespoons mustard seed
2 tablespoons celery seed
2 teaspoons turmeric
½ teaspoon ground cloves

Scrub cucumbers and slice thin. Do not peel. Cut onion into thin slices and combine with cucumbers and salt. Let stand covered at room temperature for 3 hours. Drain well. Combine remaining ingredients in a large kettle and bring to a boil. Add drained cucumbers and onion and heat thoroughly but do not boil. Pack into clean hot pint jars, leaving ⅛-inch headspace. Seal immediately. Process 5 minutes in boiling-water bath.

Kosher Dill Pickles
Makes 3 to 4 quarts

40 cucumbers, medium size
pickling variety (about 4 lbs.)
Coarse salt
3 cups white vinegar
12 cloves garlic, peeled

2 tablespoons mixed pickling
spice
4 heads fresh dill
8 small hot red peppers

Wash cucumbers thoroughly. Remove all blossoms. Soak 24 hours covered in a brine made of 1 cup salt to 8 cups water. Remove cucumber from brine, drain and pat dry. Mix vinegar and 5 cups of water in a large kettle. Tie garlic and pickling spice in a cheesecloth bag; add to mixture. Bring to boil. Add cucumbers and remove kettle from heat. Place 2 peppers and 1 head dill in each clean hot quart jar. Pack cucumbers in jar. Put vinegar mixture back on heat and return to boil. Remove spice bag. Pour liquid over cucumbers being certain cucumbers are covered with liquid but leaving ½-inch headspace. Seal immediately. Process 20 minutes in boiling-water bath.

Curry Cucumber Slices
Makes 5 to 6 pints

24 medium cucumbers
½ cup coarse salt
1 teaspoon curry powder
2 cups vinegar

2½ cups sugar
¼ cup mustard seed
1 tablespoon celery seed

Wash cucumbers and cut into thin slices but do not peel. Mix together salt and 8 cups water and pour over cucumber slices. Cover and let stand 5 hours at room temperature. Drain and rinse thoroughly with cold water. Drain again. Combine remaining ingredients in a saucepan. Bring to a boil. Add cucumber slices and return to boil. Remove from heat immediately and pack into clean hot pint jars, leaving ⅛-inch headspace. Seal immediately. Process 5 minutes in boiling-water bath.

Cucumber Slices
Makes 5 to 6 pints

12 large cucumbers
6 medium onions
¼ cup coarse salt
4 cups vinegar
2 cups firmly packed light
   brown sugar

1 tablespoon dry mustard
1 tablespoon turmeric
1 tablespoon cornstarch

Wash, peel, and slice cucumbers and onions. Cover with salt and let stand covered at room temperature overnight. Combine vinegar and sugar and bring to a boil. Mix together dry mustard, turmeric and cornstarch. Combine with a little cold vinegar or water to make a paste. Add to hot vinegar mixture and bring to a boil, stirring. Drain cucumbers and onions well. Add to vinegar mixture and bring to a boil. Pack immediately into clean hot pint jars, leaving ⅛-inch headspace. Seal immediately. Process 5 minutes in boiling-water bath.

Quick Cucumber Pickles
Makes about 6 pints

4 quarts thinly sliced
   cucumbers (unpeeled)
1½ cups thinly sliced onion
⅓ cup coarse salt
2 cloves garlic, peeled
8 cups crushed ice

4 cups sugar
1½ teaspoons ground turmeric
1½ teaspoons celery seed
2 tablespoons mustard seed
3 cups white vinegar

Combine cucumbers, onion, salt and garlic in a large crock or bowl. Cover the top with crushed ice and let stand 3 hours. Drain mixture thoroughly, discard liquid. If desired, discard garlic cloves as well. Combine sugar, turmeric, celery seed, mustard seed and vinegar in a kettle. Bring mixture to a boil and stir until all sugar is dissolved. Add drained vegetables and bring to a boil. Simmer, uncovered, 5 minutes. Pack into clean hot pint jars, leaving ⅛-inch headspace. Seal immediately. Process 5 minutes in boiling-water bath.

Green Tomato Pickles
Makes 3 to 4 pints

16 cups sliced green tomatoes
  (about 6 pounds)
¼ cup coarse salt
½ tablespoon powdered alum
  (optional)
3 cups vinegar (5% acidity)
4 cups sugar

1 tablespoon mixed
  pickling spices
½ teaspoon cinnamon
1 tablespoon celery seed
½ teaspoon whole allspice
1 tablespoon mustard seed

Wash tomatoes and cut into slices. Sprinkle with salt and let stand covered overnight at room temperature. Drain well. Combine 8 cups of boiling water with the powdered alum and pour over tomatoes. Let stand 20 minutes. Drain and cover with cold water. Drain again. Combine vinegar, 1 cup water, and sugar. Tie spices in cheesecloth and add to mixture. Bring to a boil. Pour over tomatoes, cover and let stand overnight. Drain liquid from tomatoes into a saucepan and bring to a boil. Pour hot mixture back over tomatoes. Cover and let stand overnight. The next morning bring tomatoes and mixture to a boil. Pack into clean hot pint jars, leaving ⅛-inch headspace. Seal immediately. Process 5 minutes in boiling-water bath.

Crabapple Pickles
Makes 5 to 6 pints

8 pounds crabapples
4 cups vinegar
4 cups sugar
1 tablespoon whole cloves

1 stick cinnamon
1 teaspoon whole allspice
1 teaspoon whole mace

Wash crabapples and sort for uniform size. Do not peel. Combine vinegar, 3 cups water, and sugar in a large saucepan. Tie spices in cheesecloth. Add to mixture and bring to a boil. Cool. Add crabapples and heat very slowly, being careful not to burst skin of fruit. Cover and allow to stand in syrup overnight at room temperature. Next morning remove spice bag and pack apples into clean hot pint jars. Fill with syrup, leaving ½-inch headspace. Seal immediately. Process 20 minutes in boiling-water bath.

Pickled Sweet Carrots
Makes about 4 pints

8 cups sliced carrots
  (about 2 pounds)
2 cups cider vinegar
2 cups sugar

1 tablespoon whole cloves
1 tablespoon whole allspice
2 sticks cinnamon

Peel and slice carrots into ¾-inch long pieces. Cover and cook in a small amount of boiling salted water about 5 minutes or until just tender. Drain. Combine vinegar, 1½ cups water and sugar in a kettle. Add spices tied in cheesecloth. Bring mixture to a boil. Add carrots, cover, and let stand at room temperature overnight. Bring to a boil, reduce heat and simmer, uncovered, 3 minutes. Remove spices and pack carrots into clean hot pint jars. Fill to within ½ inch of top with hot syrup. Seal immediately. Process 10 minutes in boiling-water bath.

Watermelon Pickles
Makes about 4 quarts

Rind of 1 large or 2 small
  watermelon
Salt
8 cups sugar

4 cups cider vinegar
2 tablespoons whole cloves
5 sticks cinnamon
2 tablespoons whole allspice

Peel and remove all green, red and pink portions from watermelon rind. Cut rind into 1-inch cubes or slices. Cover and soak at room temperature overnight in a salt solution made from ¼ cup salt to 4 cups water. Next day drain thoroughly. Cover with clean, cold water and simmer until rind is almost tender. Drain thoroughly. Combine sugar and vinegar in large kettle. Tie spices in cheesecloth and add to mixture. Bring to a boil and simmer, uncovered, 5 minutes. Let mixture cool about 15 minutes. Add drained watermelon rind and simmer until rind is clear and translucent. Discard spice bag. Pack immediately into clean hot pint jars, leaving ⅛-inch headspace. Seal immediately. Process 5 minutes in boiling-water bath.

Dilled Green Bean Pickles
Makes about 4 pints

2 pounds fresh, crisp green beans
Salt
4 cups cider vinegar
1 cup sugar

2 tablespoons mixed
  pickling spice
2 cloves garlic, peeled
4 heads fresh dill

Sort beans and wash in cool water. Snip off tops and remove strings, if necessary. Leave beans whole. Soak in ice water 30 minutes. Make a brine of 1 tablespoon salt to 4 cups water and bring to a boil. Drain beans and add to hot brine. Simmer, covered, about 20 minutes or until just tender. Drain thoroughly. Combine vinegar and sugar in a saucepan. Tie spices in cheesecloth and add to mixture with garlic. Add beans and simmer, uncovered, 10 minutes. Pack beans standing upright into clean hot pint jars. Cover with hot vinegar mixture, leaving ½-inch headspace. Place dill in top of each jar. Seal immediately. Process 5 minutes in boiling-water bath.

Pickled Beets
Makes about 3 quarts

9 pounds tiny fresh beets
1 teaspoon whole cloves
1 teaspoon whole allspice

2 sticks cinnamon
2 cups sugar
2 cups cider vinegar

Wash and drain beets, being careful to leave on some stem and root to prevent bleeding. Cover with boiling water and simmer, covered, about 20 minutes or until tender. Drain well. When beets are cool, remove skin, stem, and root ends. If beets are not very small, slice after peeling. Tie spices in cheesecloth, combine with remaining ingredients and 2 cups of water in a saucepan and bring to a boil. Add cooked beets and simmer, uncovered, 10 minutes. Discard spices. Pack into clean hot quart jars leaving ⅛-inch headspace. Seal immediately. Process 30 minutes in boiling-water bath.

Pickled Peaches

Makes about 2 pints

2 pounds peaches
1 cup white vinegar
2¼ cups sugar

1 stick cinnamon
½ teaspoon whole cloves

Scald peaches in boiling water and then immerse in cold water. Slip off skins. Cut in half and remove pits. Combine remaining ingredients in a kettle. Bring to a boil and boil rapidly, uncovered, 5 minutes. Reduce heat. Drop peaches in gently, a few at a time, and simmer, uncovered, until just tender. *Do not overcook*. Pack into clean hot pint jars. Cover peaches with hot syrup, leaving ½-inch headspace. Seal immediately. Process 20 minutes in boiling-water bath.

Pickled Pears

Makes about 3 quarts

3 pounds pears
2 cups white vinegar
1½ cups firmly packed
  light brown sugar

1 stick cinnamon
2 thin slices ginger root
1 tablespoon whole cloves

Peel pears. Remove blossom end but leave stem end on. If pears are very firm, parboil 5 minutes in water to cover. Drain and reserve liquid for syrup. Combine 2 cups of the liquid or 2 cups water with remaining ingredients in a saucepan. Bring to a boil and boil, uncovered, 5 minutes. Add pears carefully, and simmer just until pears are transparent. Pack into clean hot quart jars. Cover fruit with hot syrup, leaving ½-inch headspace. Seal immediately. Process 20 minutes in boiling-water bath.

Green Tomato Relish
Makes about 8 pints

12 pounds green tomatoes,
  peeled and chopped
1½ cups coarse salt
1 medium head cabbage,
  chopped
12 cups (96 ounces)
  cider vinegar
6 onions, chopped
3 sweet red peppers, seeded
  and chopped

2 green peppers, seeded
  and chopped
7 cups sugar
2 tablespoons celery seed
2 tablespoons mustard seed
1 tablespoon ground cinnamon
1 tablespoon ground cloves
1 teaspoon turmeric
1 clove garlic, peeled

Sprinkle chopped tomatoes with salt, cover and let stand at room temperature overnight. Drain thoroughly and place tomatoes in large kettle. Add cabbage and vinegar. Bring to a boil and simmer 30 minutes. Add remaining ingredients and cook until thick, stirring occasionally. Remove garlic clove. Ladle into hot sterilized jars. Seal immediately.

Combination Relish
Makes about 8 pints

4 cups chopped onion
  (about 4 onions)
4 cups finely chopped cabbage
  (about 1 pound)
4 cups chopped, peeled green
  tomatoes (about 6)
6 hot red peppers, chopped
12 green peppers,
  finely chopped

½ cup coarse salt
2 cups finely chopped celery
  (about 4 stalks)
4 cups sugar
4 cups (32 ounces)
  cider vinegar
1 tablespoon celery seed
2 tablespoons mustard seed
1½ tablespoons turmeric

Combine onion, cabbage, tomatoes and peppers. Sprinkle with salt and let stand covered at room temperature overnight. Drain well the next day. Combine remaining ingredients in a kettle, add 2 cups water and bring to a boil. Simmer, uncovered, 4 to 5 minutes. Add drained vegetables. Bring to boil and simmer 10 minutes, stirring occasionally. Ladle into hot sterilized jars. Seal immediately.

Apple Chutney
Makes about 4 pints

13 tart apples, pared and
   cored (about 4 pounds)
3 green peppers, seeded
1 medium onion
1½ cups seedless raisins
1 tablespoon salt

3 cups (24 ounces) vinegar
1½ cups sugar
1½ tablespoons ground ginger
1½ cups tart grape jelly
¾ cup lemon juice
1 tablespoon grated lemon rind

Put apples, peppers, onions and raisins through food chopper using coarse blade. Place in large saucepan and add remaining ingredients. Simmer, uncovered, about 1 hour, or until mixture is thick, stirring occasionally. Ladle into hot sterilized jars. Seal immediately.

Cranberry Relish
Makes 2 to 3 pints

1 pound fresh cranberries
1 medium orange
1 cup seedless raisins
1 onion, chopped
½ cup chopped green pepper
1 clove garlic, minced
2 tablespoons minced
   fresh ginger

1 cup cider vinegar
1 can (6 ounces) frozen
   cranberry juice concentrate
2 cups sugar
½ teaspoon coarse salt
¼ teaspoon cayenne pepper
¼ teaspoon ground cloves
1 teaspoon mustard seed

Wash and sort cranberries. Put through food chopper using coarse blade. Put in large kettle. Remove orange peel from orange with a vegetable peeler, making sure not to include any white membrane. Cut peel in slivers and add to cranberries. Remove all white membrane from orange, section orange and add to cranberries. Add raisins, onion, green pepper, garlic, ginger, vinegar and cranberry juice. Bring to a boil, stirring occasionally. Boil, uncovered, 10 minutes. Add remaining ingredients. Bring to a boil and simmer, uncovered, stirring often, about 20 minutes, or until mixture becomes thick. Ladle into clean hot pint jars, leaving ⅛-inch headspace. Seal immediately. Process 10 minutes in boiling-water bath.

Sweet Relish
Makes about 3 pints

8 large ripe cucumbers
¼ cup coarse salt
4 sweet red peppers,
   seeded and cored
4 large onions, quartered

1½ tablespoons celery seed
1½ tablespoons mustard seed
2½ cups sugar
1½ cups (12 ounces)
   white vinegar

Peel and slice cucumbers. Place in glass bowl. Add salt and mix well. Cover and let stand in refrigerator overnight. Drain well. Put through food chopper with peppers and onion, using coarse blade. Place chopped vegetables in kettle with remaining ingredients. Bring to a boil and simmer, uncovered, about 30 minutes, or until mixture is thickened and vegetables are cooked, stirring occasionally. Ladle into hot sterilized jars. Seal immediately.

Relish for Hot Dogs
Makes 4 to 5 pints

3 pounds green tomatoes
4 red apples
3 sweet red peppers
4 onions
1½ tablespoons coarse salt

1½ teaspoons pepper
1½ teaspoons ground cinnamon
¾ teaspoon ground cloves
2½ cups sugar
2 cups (16 ounces) white vinegar

Wash tomatoes, remove stem ends and cut in quarters. Wash apples, cut in quarters, remove core but do not peel. Wash peppers and remove seeds. Put vegetables through food chopper, using coarse blade. Combine remaining ingredients and bring to a boil in a large kettle. Add chopped vegetables and simmer, uncovered, about 30 minutes, or until thick, stirring occasionally. Ladle into hot sterilized jars. Seal immediately.

Beet Relish
Makes 5 to 6 pints

6 cups chopped, cooked beets
  (about 3 pounds)
6 cups shredded cabbage
  (about 1½ pounds)
¾ cup freshly-grated
  horseradish

3 teaspoons coarse salt
½ teaspoon freshly ground
  black pepper
3 cups (24 ounces) cider vinegar
1½ cups sugar

Combine beets, cabbage, horseradish, salt and pepper and toss thoroughly. Combine vinegar and sugar in large kettle and heat until sugar is dissolved. Bring mixture to a boil. Add vegetable mixture, return to boil and simmer, uncovered, 5 minutes. Ladle into hot sterilized jars. Seal immediately.

Corn Relish
Makes 3 to 4 pints

12 ears sweet corn
2 onions, chopped
2 sweet green peppers, chopped
1 sweet red pepper, chopped
1 cup chopped cabbage
  (about ¼ pound)

2 tablespoons coarse salt
¼ teaspoon pepper
1½ tablespoons dry mustard
1 cup sugar
2 cups vinegar

Cut uncooked corn from cob, but do not scrape ear. Mix corn kernels with onion, pepper and cabbage in a large saucepan. Add remaining ingredients. Simmer, uncovered, about 30 minutes, or until mixture is well blended and vegetables are tender. Pack into clean hot pint jars, leaving ⅛-inch headspace. Seal immediately. Process 15 minutes in boiling-water bath.

Piccalilli
Makes 5 to 6 pints

2 sweet red peppers,
  seeded and chopped
2 green peppers,
  seeded and chopped
4 cups chopped green tomatoes
  (about 6)
1 cup chopped celery
  (about 2 stalks)

2 large onions, chopped
1 small head cabbage, chopped
½ cup coarse salt
3 cups cider vinegar
1 teaspoon dry mustard
2¼ cups firmly packed
  light brown sugar
1 teaspoon turmeric

Layer peppers, tomatoes, celery, onion and cabbage, sprinkling each layer with salt. Let mixture stand covered at room temperature overnight. The next day drain thoroughly. Put mixture in a large kettle and add the remaining ingredients. Bring to a boil and simmer, uncovered, 15 to 20 minutes, stirring frequently. Ladle into clean hot pint jars, leaving ⅛-inch headspace. Seal immediately. Process 5 minutes in boiling-water bath.

Corn Chowchow
Makes about 6 pints

4 cups shredded cabbage
  (about 1 pound)
4 cups cauliflowerets
  (1 medium head)
5 ears fresh, raw corn
3 cups cider vinegar
1 cup seeded and chopped
  green pepper

1 cup chopped onion
1 cup sugar
2 tablespoons mustard seed
2 tablespoons celery seed
1 tablespoon dry mustard
1 tablespoon turmeric
1 tablespoon coarse salt

Combine cabbage, cauliflowerets and 3 cups of water in large saucepan. Cut corn from cobs and add to mixture with remaining ingredients. Bring to a boil, reduce heat and simmer, uncovered, 30 minutes, stirring occasionally. When mixture is thick pack into clean hot pint jars, leaving ¼-inch headspace. Seal immediately. Process 20 minutes in a boiling-water bath.

Tomato Catsup
Makes about 2 pints

1 cup (8 ounces) white vinegar
1½ teaspoons whole cloves
1½ teaspoons coarsely broken
  cinnamon sticks
1 teaspoon celery seed

8 pounds fully ripe tomatoes
1 onion, chopped
½ teaspoon cayenne pepper
1 cup sugar
3 teaspoons salt

Put vinegar, cloves, cinnamon and celery seed in saucepan. Bring to boil. Remove from heat and let stand. Scald, peel and finely chop tomatoes. Place tomatoes in large kettle with 2 cups water, onion, and cayenne pepper. Bring to a boil and boil, covered, 15 minutes. Put through a food mill, discarding skin and seeds. Return purée to kettle, add sugar. Cook over medium heat, stirring frequently, for 45 minutes or until reduced by half. Strain vinegar, discarding spices. Add with salt to tomato mixture. Simmer, uncovered, stirring almost constantly, for 30 minutes or until smooth and thick. Ladle into hot sterilized jars and seal immediately.

Hot Chili Sauce
Makes about 2 pints

4 to 5 pounds fully ripe tomatoes
1 large onion, chopped
¾ cup sugar
1¼ cups (10 ounces)
  cider vinegar
1 teaspoon crushed hot red
  pepper, seeds removed

1 teaspoon mustard seed
1 teaspoon salt
½ teaspoon ground ginger
½ teaspoon nutmeg
¼ teaspoon curry powder

Peel and coarsely chop tomatoes. There should be 8 cups. In a heavy kettle combine all ingredients. Bring to a boil. Reduce heat and simmer gently, uncovered, until very thick, about 2 hours. As mixture thickens, stir very frequently to prevent sauce from sticking and scorching. Ladle into clean hot jars and seal immediately. To keep for any length of time, process 15 minutes in boiling-water bath.

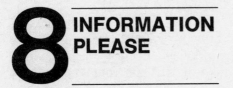

8 INFORMATION PLEASE

Q. Why is open-kettle preserving not recommended for fruit and vegetables?

A. In open-kettle preserving, food is cooked in an ordinary kettle, then packed into hot jars and sealed without processing. The temperature reached in open-kettle preserving is not high enough to destroy all spoilage organisms that may be in the food. Spoilage bacteria may get into the jar when food is transferred from kettle to jar.

Q. Should the hot pack method be used for all vegetables?

A. Yes, with the exception of tomatoes. Precooking and hot packing permit rapid heat penetration during pressure processing. This is important because of the high temperature needed to destroy spoilage organisms in non-acid vegetables.

Q. Why are both the cold and hot pack methods recommended for fruit?

A. Precooking, with hot packing, shrinks fruit and therefore more fruit can be packed in a container. The cold pack method is better for berries, because this method helps retain their natural shape.

Q. Why are foods classified as acid and low-acid?

A. The acid content of food determines how it may be preserved safely. Food with relatively high acid content like fruit, tomatoes and sauerkraut may be processed in a water-bath because boiling water temperature (212°F) is sufficient to destroy spoilage organisms in these foods. Low-acid food like meat, seafood, poultry and most vegetables except tomatoes

111

and sauerkraut, must be processed in a steam-pressure processor because a temperature of 240°F is required to destroy spoilage organisms in these foods.

Q. What causes peaches and pears to turn dark brown after they have been preserved?

A. Fruit in the top of a jar will discolour if the processing has not been long enough, or if the temperature was not high enough to render inactive the enzyme which causes discolouration or to expel air from the jar. Fruit exposed to air too long after being peeled and before being bottled may turn dark. Discolouration can be avoided if fruit is kept in lightly salted water until ready for processing. A tablespoon of lemon juice added to pears preserved by the cold pack method will help them retain their original colour. Fruit preserved without sugar sometimes turns brown after being opened and exposed to air, just as fresh fruit does when exposed to air after it has been peeled.

Q. How much salt should be added to the water in which peeled fruit is placed to prevent discolouration?

A. One teaspoon of salt to each quart of water is sufficient.

Q. Does ascorbic acid help keep fruit and vegetables from darkening?

A. Yes. The addition of ¼ teaspoon of crystalline ascorbic acid (Vitamin C) to a quart of fruit or vegetables, before processing, retards oxidation, a cause of darkening in preserved food.

Q. Why does preserved fruit sometimes float in jars?

A. Fruit may float because it is packed too loosely or the syrup is too heavy. It may also float if some air remains in the tissue of the fruit after it has been heated and processed.

Q. Why do quarts require a longer processing time than pints by the cold pack method—but not by the hot pack method?

A. When food is packed cold it takes longer for the heat to reach the center of a quart jar. With the hot pack method, food at the center of both the pint and quart is equally hot when packed.

Q. How should food be packed, loosely or firmly?

112

A. Food such as corn, peas, lima beans and greens should be packed loosely because heat penetration in these foods is difficult. Fruit and tomatoes should be firmly and solidly packed because shrinkage takes place during processing. Their texture does not retard heat penetration. A solid, but not tight, pack should be made with all other food.

Q. Must jars and lids be sterilized before preserving?

A. With open-kettle canning, jars and lids should be sterilized. When food is processed in a jar, sterilization is not required but all jars should be thoroughly washed. Lids should be covered with water and boiled five minutes. Screw bands need not be sterilized. Heating of jars helps prevent breakage when packed with hot food.

Q. How should jars be sterilized?

A. Wash jars and lids in hot suds. Rinse well in clear water. Place jars in hot water to cover. Bring to a boil and boil 20 minutes. Lids should be boiled five minutes and left in hot water until needed. If jars are removed from boiling water and allowed to stand exposed to air, the entire process of sterilization will be defeated.

Q. What does sterilizing accomplish?

A. Enzymes, yeasts, moulds and bacteria which can be the cause of food spoilage are destroyed or rendered inactive by sterilizing.

Q. Will jars that are boiled in water before preserving be toughened?

A. No. Jars are fully tempered when made and boiling will not increase their resistance to heat.

Q. What causes jars to break in a processor?

A. Breakage occurs for several reasons: the use of commercial jars instead of Mason jars; the use of old jars that have invisible hair-line cracks, or that have been subjected to a blow in shipment or handling; placing jars directly on the bottom of a cooker, instead of on a rack.

Q. What causes the milky deposit which appears on jars after they are removed from the processor?

A. Minerals that are naturally present in water, usually calcium, may leave a deposit. This deposit can be prevented by adding a tablespoon of vinegar, or a teaspoon of cream of tartar, to the water in the cooker. Vinegar will also help prevent mineral stains on the inside of the processor itself.

Q. What are half-gallon jars used for?

A. Most water-bath or steam-pressure processors are not large enough to accommodate half-gallon jars but they can be used for pickles and relishes that do not require further processing.

Q. What kinds of lids may be used?

A. There are four types of lids. The most popular is the two-piece lid which consists of a flat metal disc with sealing compound and a screw band. The metal disc must be discarded and replaced after it has been used. The screw band may be used over and over.

Q. Why must metal lids be put into boiling water for five minutes before using?

A. This procedure sterilizes the lid. It also softens the compound of which the built-in rubber ring is made, so it will "take" the imprint of the jar top and more readily fill in any slight irregularities in the sealing edge of the jar. This insures a positive seal. The rubber sealing compound on lids can be damaged if they are boiled more than five minutes.

Q. What holds metal lids in place after the screw bands are removed?

A. Two things. The built-in rubber ring forms a sort of "weld" or seal when compressed against the rim of the jar by the screw band. But of even more importance is the vacuum created in the jar as the contents cool. There is up to 10 pounds of air pressure on top of the lid helping to hold the seal.

Q. Why do the undersides of lids sometimes discolour?

A. Natural compounds in some food corrode the metal and leave a brown or black deposit on the underside of the lid. This deposit is harmless.

Q. Why do some screw bands stick to jars?

A. This is caused by food juices on jar threads. Juices

holding screw bands to the jar can be dissolved in warm water. Adhesions can also be broken by tapping screw bands lightly with a knife handle.

Q. How can you tell if the jar is actually sealed?

A. After jars have cooled for 24 hours, check the two-piece metal lids and screw bands. If the lid is depressed in the center, a satisfactory vacuum has been made, and the jar is sealed. But if the lid has not snapped down, and still remains raised in the center, it is a warning that something is interfering with a perfect seal. The jar may be too full, there might be a nick in the rim of the jar, or a food particle could be caught in the sealing edge.

Q. Should jars be turned on their sides or turned upside down to test the seal?

A. Jars sealed by vacuum should not be turned upside down unless it is necessary to distribute ascorbic acid. To do so might break the seal which has been formed.

Q. What if the seal is defective?

A. Reprocess at once, or refrigerate food and use as soon as possible.

Q. Does it matter if bubbles appear in a jar after it is taken out of the processor to cool?

A. No. Bubbles often appear in a jar after it is removed from the processor because food is still boiling in the jar. Ordinarily bubbles do not appear after the jar has been allowed to cool thoroughly.

Q. Should jars be cooled in the water-bath?

A. No. The food will overcook.

Q. Should water completely cover jars in the water bath?

A. Yes, by at least an inch. If water level drops during processing add more **boiling** water to keep jars covered.

Q. Can **Clostridium botulinum** spores be readily destroyed at boiling temperature simply by processing jars in a water-bath processor longer than in a pressure processor?

A. No. The only safe way to destroy **Clostridium botulinum** is to process under pressure so food in the jar will reach 240°F. (At sea level, 240°F is attained at

10 pounds pressure.)

Q. Are special directions required for processing at high altitudes?

A. Yes. As atmospheric pressure lessens at higher altitudes, the boiling point of water lowers. In order to compensate for this it is necessary to use a higher pressure for cooking and preserving to insure a processing temperature of 240°F. If the processor has weights, use 15 pounds instead of 10 pounds at 2,000 feet or more above sea level. If the processor has a dial gauge, pressure should be increased one pound for every 2,000 feet (or follow manufacturer's instructions).

Q. Why is a rack always used in a pressure processor or water-bath processor?

A. A rack holds jars off the bottom of the processor. Jars placed directly on the bottom of a processor may crack.

Q. Should a cover be put on the water-bath?

A. Yes. This will save fuel and keep the water at the top of the kettle boiling.

Q. How is time figured in hot or cold pack preserving?

A. With a pressure processor, start timing when the indicator on the pressure gauge reaches the required pressure (or follow manufacturer's instructions). When using a water-bath, start timing when the water surrounding the jars starts to boil.

Q. Why is processing time different for different food?

A. Processing time is determined by the rate of heat penetration through a food to the center of the jar. For example, it takes longer for heat to penetrate solid packed food like squash than it takes to penetrate peas.

Q. Processing time is always longer than cooking time. Why?

A. In preserving, food must be processed long enough, and at a high enough temperature, to kill all spoilage organisms. In cooking, food should be heated only long enough to make it tender and palatable.

Q. May acid foods be processed in a pressure processor?

A. Yes. Use five pounds instead of 10 pounds of pressure. Processing under pressure is not necessary from the standpoint of safety, but it does save time—from one third to one half less time is needed than is required in a water-bath.

Q. How is a dial gauge checked?

A. Usually it is necessary to return it to the manufacturer. However, some county extension home economists have equipment to perform this service.

Q. If preserved food appears to be overcooked, may processing time be shortened to improve the look and the taste of the food?

A. No. If processing time is shortened, food probably will not be safe to eat.

Q. What about oven processing?

A. This is an old-fashioned method no longer recommended, because the temperature of the food in the jars does not get high enough to destroy all spoilage organisms. In addition, jars may seal during processing and explode, damaging the oven and possibly injuring people.

Q. Why is *botulism* of concern to preserved food, but not of concern when food is cooked for immediate use?

A. *Clostridium botulinum* is an anaerobic bacterium, which means it thrives only in the absence of air. As a result, a sealed jar of low-acid food is the perfect place for the spores to grow. Food prepared for immediate consumption does not present an opportunity for the spores to develop and produce a toxin.

Q. What causes liquid to be lost from jars during processing?

A. Jar may be packed too full or too tight: Allow headspace of ½ inch to 1 inch between the top of the food and the lid. Since food and liquid expand when boiled, headspace must be adequate or liquid will be forced out.

Trapped air bubbles in jar may not have been released: After jar is filled with food and liquid, and before cover is put on, a clean table knife should be run down the inside of the jar in several places to release trapped air bubbles. If this is not done, liquid may be forced out when food begins to boil.

Pressure during processing may have fluctuated.

Hastening the reduction of pressure after processing may also cause liquid to be lost: Cooker should be removed from the heat and allowed to cool normally at room temperature. Don't run water over the cooker or set the cooker in cold water. Don't place it on a cold surface or in a draft. Don't nudge the control frequently to test for pressure. Any of these things may cause pressure to drop more quickly in the cooker than in the jars, forcing liquid out of the jars. Simply remove cooker from heat and, after 20 or 25 minutes, nudge control to check pressure. After this length of time, pressure is usually down and the control and cover can be removed.

Q. If liquid is lost from jars during processing, can more water be added to fill them again?

A. No, not unless you plan to process the jars all over again. If the seal is broken and anything is added to the jar, bacteria may be introduced and complete reprocessing will be necessary. If correct procedures are followed, food in jars from which liquid has been lost will be safe to eat, even if the food looks different from food that is covered with liquid.

Q. Can fruit and vegetables be preserved without heating if aspirin is used instead of heat?

A. *No.* Aspirin cannot be used to prevent spoilage. Adequate heat treatment is the only safe procedure.

Q. Is it all right to use preservatives in home preserving?

A. *No.* Some canning powders and chemical preservatives are harmful.

Q. How long should home-preserved food be kept?

A. It is recommended that it be eaten within a year, before it loses its fine flavour. Few homes have adequate storage space for quantities larger than a year's supply and most food can be replenished each year.

Q. What causes preserved food to spoil?

A. Spoilage is caused by moulds, yeasts, bacteria and enzymes. When there is insufficient sterilization, incomplete seal of containers, lack of care in handling food and equipment, when containers are allowed to stand and cool before processing, or containers are cooled too slowly after processing, these spoilage agents may remain active.

Q. How does heat or cold affect preserved foods?

A. Excessive heat may destroy the seal of the jar by causing expansion of the contents. Warm storage encourages rapid growth of microorganisms. Freezing and thawing injures the flavour and texture of preserved food.

Q. Is it safe to use home preserved food if the liquid is cloudy?

A. Cloudy liquid may be a sign of spoilage. But it may also be caused by the minerals in hard water or by starch from overripe vegetables. If liquid is cloudy, boil the food. *Do not taste or use any food that foams during heating or any food that has a strange odour.*

Q. Are cloudy peas always a sign of spoilage?

A. No, not necessarily. If there is no bad odour or other sign of spoilage, the cloudiness is probably due either to overprocessing or the use of peas which are too mature.

Q. Can spoiled food always be detected by changes in appearance, odour or taste?

A. No, not always. Improperly preserved food does not necessarily look or smell bad. On the other hand, some changes in colour may naturally occur in food which has been properly preserved. Home-preservers who use the correct methods need not worry about safety. Doubtful food should be boiled vigorously in an open saucepan at least 10 or 20 minutes before it is tasted.

Q. What is the meaning of "flat-sour"?

A. "Flat-sour" is spoilage caused by bacteria that gives food a sour taste.

Q. What causes "flat-sour"?

A. "Flat-sour" is usually caused by preserving overripe food or by allowing precooked food to stand in jars too long before processing. This may result in the growth of organisms that produce acid (sour) but no gas (flat). It may also be caused by cooling jars too slowly after processing. It is an indication of food spoilage. To prevent "flat-sour," use fresh produce and process, cool and store properly.

Q. May food be preserved without salt? Without sugar?

A. Yes. Salt and sugar are used only for flavour and may be omitted for dietary purposes.

Q. Will pieces of food be injured if they touch the lid?

A. No.

Q. What makes preserved food change colour?

A. Darkening of food at the top of a jar may be caused by oxidation due to air in the jar. It may also be caused by inadequate heating or processing which has not destroyed enzymes. Overprocessing may cause discolouration of food throughout the container. Pink and blue colours, sometimes seen in preserved pears, apples and peaches, are caused by chemical changes in the colouring matter of fruit.

Iron and copper from cooking utensils, or from some water, may cause brown, black and grey colours in some foods.

When preserved corn turns brown, the discolouring may be due to the variety of corn used, to the stage of ripeness, or to overprocessing.

Q. Should preserved vegetables be recooked before being tasted or eaten?

A. *Yes.* Vegetables should be removed from jar, placed in a saucepan with preserving liquid, brought to a boil, uncovered, and boiled vigorously for at least 10 minutes.

Q. Why does food occasionally spoil after months of storage?

A. Although this rarely happens, spoilage is sometimes caused by a storage place that is too warm. In addition, occasionally particles of food lodge on the edge of a jar and become part of the seal. As the food particles gradually disintegrate, a tiny opening is made which permits air to enter the jar.

120

Q. Why should food be stored in a dark, cool place?

A. Light discolours food and destroys riboflavin. To retain the best flavour, food should be stored in a dark place where the temperature is between 50° and 60°F.

Q. Why does jelly sometimes fail to set?

A. There may be several reasons: use of overripe fruit or of fruit lacking in pectin; too short a boiling time before or after adding sugar; use of too much sugar in proportion to pectin and acid in the fruit juice; weather! Jelly should not be made on a very damp day. Note: Sometimes jelly does not completely set until the second or third day.

Q. What makes jelly tough?

A. If the juice is boiled too long after adding sugar or if there is too little sugar in proportion to the pectin and acid in the juice, jelly may be tough. Some fruit, such as currants and crabapples, which are high in pectin and acid, require a high proportion of sugar to make a tender jelly. If more water is added to these fruits, a smaller amount of sugar may be used.

Q. Why is jelly not always clear?

A. Clouded jelly may result from: squeezing the jelly bag which forces particles of fruit into juice; using too great a proportion of underripe fruit; incomplete removal of scum from the jelly before pouring into jelly glasses.

Q. What makes jelly "weep"?

A. Weeping is usually caused by too much acid in the fruit juice. It may be prevented by mixing a juice high in acid with a juice low in acid.

Q. What makes crystals form in jelly?

A. Sugar crystals may result from any one of four different causes: an excess of sugar; insufficient acid; overcooking; too long a delay in sealing.

Note: *Crystals in grape jelly may be greatly reduced by allowing the juice to stand for several hours in a cold place before making the jelly. The crystals will settle to the bottom of the container and the juice may be poured off.*

9 FREEZING FOOD

Freezing is a quick, easy, and convenient way to preserve food with much of its natural colour, texture, flavour, and nutritive value. There are many advantages to freezing food at home. It provides an opportunity to preserve food from the garden and to buy food in season, or on sale, that can be used many months later when the same food is more expensive. The use of frozen food is also a time-saver. Most frozen food can be readied for the table more quickly than fresh food because it is already partially prepared.

HOW FREEZING PRESERVES FOOD

Food spoils as a result of the action of microorganisms and enzymes, a complex group of chemicals that are found naturally in food. When food is canned, heat is applied to the food in jars and this process destroys or inactivates the spoilage agents. When food is frozen, the low temperature inactivates or retards the activity of the bacteria and enzymes that cause food to spoil. Freezing does not necessarily destroy the microorganisms, yeasts, moulds, and bacteria. The low temperature just makes them dormant. But they are still present, ready to spring into action as soon as the temperature of the food rises, as it does when food is thawed. In addition, ice crystals that form in frozen food rupture cells and, as a result, thawed food may soften and be penetrated more easily by food spoilage organisms than fresh food. For this reason, all food to be frozen should be in excellent condition. Remember, when food is removed from the freezer, it will not be in better condition than when it was placed there. Once food has been picked or purchased, it should be handled with speed and efficiency and processed under strict sanitary conditions.

Enzymes

Freezing retards the activity of enzymes, but does not stop it completely. Therefore, when vegetables are to be frozen, it is necessary to begin by immersing them briefly in boiling water, a process called blanching or scalding. This process inactivates enzymes. Blanching also deepens the natural colour of vegetables and makes them softer and easier to pack. When blanching is omitted, vegetables may change colour, develop undesirable flavours, and become over-soft and inedible.

PACKAGING

Frozen food must be properly wrapped to keep moisture in and air out. Improperly packaged food dries out during storage, and the result is a condition know as freezer burn. There is also a lowering of quality, flavour, texture, and nutritive value. Be sure to select moisture- and vapour-proof materials to wrap food for storage. This will prevent the flow of water, or water vapour, from food to the dry air of the freezer and will therefore prevent food from drying out. It will also prevent food from absorbing the flavours of other food.

Mason Jars

Some of the Mason jars used in canning are also suitable as freezer containers because they are leak-proof and vapour-proof and have the added advantage of allowing you to see easily what is stored. Since not all jars are safe to use in the freezer, it is necessary to check the manufacturer's instructions regarding the use of specific jars. If in doubt, you can make a simple test to determine whether or not the jars you have on hand are suitable containers for freezing food. Fill a jar with water, leaving at least 1½ inches headspace for expansion. Secure the lid. Put the jar in a plastic bag, in case it breaks, and place the filled jar in the freezer. Leave it there for two or three days. Remove the jar from the freezer and defrost it. If the glass does not break or crack it probably is safe for freezer use. Check to be sure the caps are rustproof and provide an airtight seal.

Rigid Plastic Containers

There are many types of rigid plastic containers available, and they come in a wide variety of shapes and sizes. These containers are leakproof and particularly well suited for food packed with syrup or sauce. They are reusable and can double as refrigerator dishes.

Headspace

Food expands as it freezes. Therefore, when food is tightly packed in rigid containers, it is necessary to leave headspace. Leave 1½ inches headspace in glass jars and about ½ inch headspace in rigid plastic containers. Slightly more headspace is necessary for fruit packed in syrup. Fruit and vegetables packed whole, or cut into large pieces, require less headspace than the same product cut into small pieces. Failure to leave adequate headspace will cause the top of the container to lift off, permitting air to enter the package. It may also cause glass jars to crack or break.

Plastic or Polyethylene Bags

Polyethylene or heavy plastic freezer bags are flexible and adapt easily to irregularly shaped food such as meat, poultry, and fish. They are also excellent for use in packaging blanched vegetables and small fruit such as berries. Air should be pressed out of the bag after it has been filled. The neck of the bag should be twisted several times to seal it, then doubled over to form a gooseneck and secured with a twist tie. If the bag does not tear, it can be washed, dried, and reused several times. Coloured plastic bags can be used over packaged or wrapped food to help organize the freezer. Select a variety of colours and code them for different kinds of food. Most food should be wrapped in meal-size packages, although large bags may be used for storing vegetables and berries that have been "individually frozen" (frozen on a cookie sheet).

Be sure to use plastic bags specifically designed for freezing. Sandwich bags and other lightweight refrigerator bags are not moisture- and vapour-proof and are not heavy enough to protect food properly.

Other Wrapping Material

Special wax-coated freezer wrap is available in rolls. This wrapping material can be cut to the size of the food to be packaged. The "drugstore" fold or wrap is particularly good with this kind of material because the interlocking folds at the centre and the ends of the package help prevent moisture loss. The folds should be covered with special freezer tape for extra protection.

Heavy duty aluminum foil is often used as a wrap because it conforms easily to the shape of the food being wrapped. There is the added advantage that food may be taken from the freezer and cooked in the foil wrap. It is important to be sure the foil does not tear and expose the food to air while it is in the freezer. Foil should not be used for salted or brined foods such as bacon or ham because the salt will pit the foil and cause holes which will allow air to enter the package. If foil is used for these products, they must be prewrapped in plastic before they are wrapped in foil.

All plastic wrap must be moisture- and vapour-proof, heavy, and easily sealed. Wax paper, butcher paper, and store wrappings are not suitable for use in the freezer and will not protect frozen food during storage. Pre-packaged food must be over-wrapped or rewrapped with a suitable packaging material.

Freezer Tape

Select freezer tape designed to stick at low temperatures. Gummed paper or Scotch tape will not seal frozen food packages satisfactorily. The correct tape is important because, if a package comes unsealed, air can enter the package and the quality of the food will be seriously affected.

Labelling

Label each package with a waterproof marker. When labels are used they must stick at freezer temperatures. Indicate contents, date packaged, date by which food must be used, weight or number of portions, and future use for food (pies, jams, jellies, desserts, etc.). Use tie tag labels and a waterproof marker for plastic bags, or write in pencil so the tags can be erased and reused.

EQUIPMENT

The equipment needed to process food for the freezer usually can be found in most reasonably well equipped kitchens. You will need such things as vegetable brushes, paring and chopping knives, measuring cups and spoons, bowls and paper towels.

The Blancher

One particularly handy piece of equipment for processing vegetables is a blancher. This is a utensil similar to a double boiler. The difference is that the top half is perforated. When there is enough water in the bottom section to cover the food in the perforated upper half, the pot serves as a blancher. When the water in the bottom half is below the basket, the pot serves as a steamer. It is easy to improvise a blancher by using a large, deep saucepan and a wire basket or inexpensive steamer basket. This equipment is used for blanching vegetables, a procedure necessary to inactivate enzymes. It may also be used to blanch fruit such as peaches or tomatoes so skins can be removed easily. In addition, it can double as a steamer for cooking fresh or frozen vegetables, allowing them to retain many of the nutrients lost when vegetables are cooked in water.

Thermometers

In order to protect food in the freezer, a temperature of 0°F or –10°F must be maintained at all times. There is no way you can check the temperature in your freezer unless you use a freezer thermometer. One particularly effective model can be read without opening the freezer because the temperature indicator sits outside, attached to the side of the freezer. This thermometer can be very helpful if the power should fail because you can monitor the temperature inside the freezer without opening the door, something you should never do during a power failure.

"INDIVIDUALLY FROZEN" PRODUCE

Some produce can be "individually frozen" and then packaged and stored. Process vegetables or berries, drain on paper towels, and place in a single layer on a cookie sheet. Cover with plastic wrap and set in the coldest part of the freezer. When food has been completely frozen, pour it into moisture- and vapour-proof polyethylene bags. Seal, label, and store.

Berries and vegetables frozen this way will not stick to each other in a solid mass. A specific amount can be removed from the bag, which should be resealed and returned to the freezer. However, air enters the bag each time it is opened, so it is advisable to store only enough for two or three meals in each bag.

FREEZERS

The only major investment necessary to enjoy the benefits of home freezing is a freezer. And once a freezer has been purchased, it's important to learn how to use it properly and economically. A well-stocked freezer is more economical to operate than a substantially empty one. But it doesn't make sense to stockpile food during the summer harvest without regard to the needs of the family or a plan regarding how and when the food will be used. Using food at random, without giving proper thought to maximum safe storage time, can be a waste of time, effort and money.

Proper use of a freezer is very much like the proper operation of a small store. It requires discipline and year-round involvement. When you place food in the freezer, it's a good idea to make an inventory of the food on a chart and keep it close by. As you use the food you can check it off the chart. In this way you will always know exactly what food you have on hand and what replacements should be made. The most economical way to keep a freezer well stocked is to take advantage of low cost, seasonal fruit and vegetables and supermarket sales. Check local papers for weekly bargains but remember, no matter how inexpensive an item is, it's no bargain if it's a food the family doesn't enjoy eating. Keep a close check on the food stocked in your freezer, as well as the date by which the food should be eaten. This will make meal planning easier and ensure the use of food while it is still at its best.

Choosing a Freezer

Food must be stored in a freezer at a temperature of 0°F to –10°F or lower. There are three kinds of freezers available that are capable of maintaining this temperature: the upright freezer, the chest freezer, and refrigerator-freezer combinations. Refrigerators with a small inside freezing compartment are not cold enough for long term storage. All types of freezers come in regular models that must be defrosted manually and in no-frost models that defrost automatically.

Upright Freezers

Upright freezers are easy to load and to keep organized. Each shelf can be loaded separately or reserved for specific items, and you can see at a glance what is available. Although upright models require less floor space than chest models, they are slightly more expensive to operate. Each time the door of an upright is opened, warm air rushes in and cold air tumbles out. The amount of cold air lost is greater than the amount lost by a chest model. As a result, slightly more electricity is required to maintain the correct temperature. Properly cared for, freezers of any type that are not overloaded should not need manual defrosting more than twice a year. However, upright models that defrost automatically use more electricity for the defrosting process than chest models because of the extra loss of cold air when opened.

Chest Freezers

Chest freezers that are defrosted manually are the most inexpensive models to operate. They have very few interior shelves or baskets and therefore accommodate slightly more food per cubic foot than upright freezers. It is somewhat easier to store large bulky items like turkeys and large cuts of meat in a chest model than in an upright. On the other hand, it is much more difficult to organize the contents of a

128

chest freezer or to reach packages stored at the bottom. It can be very difficult to keep track of food and to rotate it properly. Try to place heavy bulky items on the bottom. Put lighter weight food that may damage easily, or small packages that may get lost, on top or in a basket. Food must be rotated when the freezer is restocked to be certain that none is left in the freezer longer than the time recommended for safe storage.

Refrigerator-Freezer Combinations

To provide safe and proper storage for frozen food, a refrigerator-freezer combination must have separate doors and separate controls for each compartment. Models that do not have separate doors and controls cannot be used for long term storage of food because the freezer compartment cannot be maintained at temperatures low enough for safe storage. In addition, most combination models, even those with separate controls, don't provide enough storage space for extensive home freezing projects. You will need one cubic foot of storage space to accommodate approximately thirty-five pounds of food. If the only freezer space you have available is in a refrigerator-freezer combination, you will have to allocate some of the space for ice cubes and short term storage. The space that remains will probably be too limited to permit adequate circulation of air around food during the first twenty-four hours of storage when the food is being frozen.

Loading the Freezer

Familiarize yourself with the information provided in the "Use and Care" booklet that usually accompanies a freezer. Follow the directions and recommendations in the booklet for loading your particular model.

Place wrapped food in the coldest part of the freezer, leaving enough space between packages for air to circulate freely around each package. You will need one cubic foot of space for every two or three pounds of food during the initial freezing period. Don't prepare more food for the freezer than can be frozen properly within twenty-four hours. If the freezer is overloaded, the temperature will rise and the rate at which the food freezes will be slowed down.

This may also adversely affect the quality of all other food stored in the freezer. After twenty-four hours, the newly frozen food may be moved and stored in any section of the freezer. Remember, food that freezes too slowly will be inferior in quality and may even spoil.

Defrosting the Freezer

A build-up of frost in the freezer insulates food and keeps it warmer than it would be if frost were not present. In addition, the more frost present in a freezer, the more electricity required to maintain the correct temperature. Therefore, it is important to defrost the freezer whenever frost builds up beyond three-quarters of an inch. In a properly operated freezer this should be about twice a year. Plan to defrost before you restock and, if possible, do it on a cool day. Remove food from the freezer and insulate it well with blankets. Turn off freezer and place several pans of hot water inside. As ice loosens it should be removed. When all the frost has been removed, wash the interior with a solution of water and baking soda (⅓ cup of baking soda to 5 cups of water). Wipe dry and turn on freezer. Allow about thirty minutes for temperature to drop and then return food to freezer.

Frequent opening of the freezer door creates frost build-up because warm, moist air flows into the freezer every time the door is opened. To avoid frequent defrosting, plan ahead and try to avoid opening the door unnecessarily.

Loss of Power

When the electricity goes off, the freezer goes off too. When this happens *do not open the freezer!* It is vitally important to keep as much cold air as possible inside the freezer. When the electricity goes back on, check the contents of the freezer. If the food is still frozen you have no problem. If some of the food has begun to defrost, but is still cold, it may be refrozen safely, but the quality may have been impaired. If the food is warm it must be cooked immediately or discarded entirely. Food that has been frozen uncooked, thawed, and then cooked, may be refrozen safely.

FREEZING FRUIT

Fruit to be frozen is divided into two groups: fruit that discolours when exposed to oxygen and fruit that does not. Fruit that discolours must be pitted or peeled before freezing and usually is packed in a dry sugar pack or a sugar syrup. This group includes apples, peaches, pears, apricots, cherries and plums. Fruits that do not discolour are suitable for dry pack freezing (sugarless pack), and may be packed whole. This group includes most small fruits such as cranberries, raspberries, strawberries, blueberries, currants and rhubarb.

Some varieties of fruit are better for freezing than others. In order to find out which fruits are most suitable, it's a good idea to run a test by freezing a small amount. If the results are satisfactory, you can process the fruit in greater quantity.

All fruit to be frozen must be fully ripe, but not over-ripe, and should be processed as soon as possible after the fruit has been picked. Choose fruit that has ripened evenly throughout and which is uniform in both size and shape.

Preventing Discolouration

There are three ways to prevent discolouration of fruit: processing in a brine bath, packing with sugar or syrup, and adding ascorbic acid (vitamin C).

Brine Bath: A brine bath is made by mixing one teaspoon of salt with five cups of cold water. Fruit is dropped into the brine bath immediately after peeling or pitting. It is allowed to soak for fifteen or twenty minutes, but no longer or the fruit will develop a salty taste. Fruit should be drained and rinsed in ice-cold water before packing. A fresh brine bath must be made for a new batch of fruit if the water discolours.

Packing with sugar or syrup: Sugar or syrup packed with fruit before freezing helps prevent discolouration because it slows the action of the enzymes responsible for browning. It also protects fruit from air and helps preserve colour, texture, and flavour.

Ascorbic Acid: Ascorbic acid, mixed with dry sugar prior to packing or dissolved in the syrup in which fruit is packed, provides added protection against discolouration.

Packing

There are several ways to pack fruit. The correct pack depends on the type of fruit to be frozen, whether it will discolour easily, how tart it is, and its ultimate use. Fruit to be used in pies may be frozen without sugar. Fruit that will ultimately be used to make jam or jelly must be frozen without sugar. It should be measured carefully before freezing, and the weight or volume marked on the container. An exact amount of fruit is usually required for a recipe, and the volume of fresh fruit differs from that of defrosted fruit. Fruit that is to be stewed or eaten without further preparation after thawing may be packed in a sugar syrup. For additional flavour, or a low calorie pack, some fruits or fruit cocktails may be packaged in unsweetened fruit juice.

Dry or Sugarless Pack

Small, whole fruit such as raspberries, currants, cranberries or blueberries may be frozen without sugar. Apples or peaches to be used in pies may be dipped in a brine bath, cooled, and then frozen without sugar.

Sugar Pack

Select soft fruits such as raspberries, strawberries, peaches or apricots that yield juice when they have been mixed with sugar and allowed to stand ten to fifteen minutes. Add ¼ teaspoon of ascorbic acid to each cup of sugar (or follow instructions on the package) when packing fruit that discolours easily. Place prepared fruit in a bowl and toss gently with sugar. Allow fruit to stand ten to fifteen minutes, or until sugar has dissolved in juice. Pack fruit in glass or rigid containers. Leave recommended headspace, seal, label and freeze.

Syrup Pack

Type of Syrup	Sugar	Water	Approximate Syrup Yield
Very light	1 cup	4 cups	4½ cups
Light	1 cup	3 cups	3½ cups
Medium	1 cup	2 cups	2¼ cups
Heavy	1 cup	1 cup	1½ cups

Dissolve sugar in warm water. Chill. Add ⅛ teaspoon ascorbic acid to each cup of sugar (follow instructions on the package). Allow ⅔ to 1 cup of syrup for each pint container, or enough syrup to cover fruit.

Prepare fruit. (Remember to process light-coloured fruit in a brine bath.) Pack in containers, leaving 1 to 2 inches headspace. Add chilled syrup, leaving ¾-inch headspace in quart containers and ½-inch headspace in pint containers. Remove air by gently inserting a clean knife between container and fruit. Wipe sealing edge and seal. A piece of crumpled wax paper may be placed over fruit to hold it under the syrup. Label container and freeze.

Low Calorie Sweeteners

If you prefer to use a low calorie sweetener instead of sugar, write to the manufacturer for information concerning the use of the product in freezing fruit. Check with your physician to be sure you may safely use a low calorie sweetener this way.

Freezing

Place sealed, labeled containers in the coldest part of the freezer as soon as possible after processing. Leave space for cold air to circulate around each package. Allow twenty-four hours for proper freezing, then transfer containers to any convenient location in the freezer.

Using Frozen Fruit

The most popular way to serve fruit that has been frozen is to serve it partially defrosted and uncooked. Frozen fruit deteriorates rapidly as it defrosts; therefore, it is advisable to defrost just before serving. Defrost in an unopened container in the refrigerator. If there is an emergency, the container may be placed briefly in warm water to speed thawing. Fruit that is to be stewed should be partially defrosted before cooking to ensure even heat penetration during cooking. Fruit that is to be used in pies should be partially defrosted before it is placed in the crust so the fruit filling can be spread easily and cook simultaneously with crust. This will also prevent the bottom crust from getting soggy.

FRUIT PREPARATION CHART

Fruit	For Use In	Type of Pack	Preparation
Apples	Pies. (Defrost slightly to prevent soggy crust.)	Dry or sugarless pack.	Wash, peel and core. Cut into eighths and drop into brine bath. Pack in rigid containers, leaving 1 inch headspace.
Applesauce	Cakes, cookies, desserts or "as is."	Applesauce may be sweetened to taste or left unsweetened.	Prepare applesauce using your favourite recipe. Pack in rigid containers, leaving ½-inch headspace.
Apricots	Desserts.	Thin or medium syrup pack. Add ascorbic acid.	Wash and pit. Cut in halves or quarters. Drop into brine bath. Pack in rigid containers; pour syrup over, leaving 1 inch headspace.
	Pies or cooked desserts.	Dry sugar pack: ⅔ cup sugar to 4 cups fruit. Add ascorbic acid.	Wash and pit. Cut in halves or quarters. Pack in rigid containers, leaving ½-inch headspace.
Blueberries	Pancakes, muffins, pies, desserts and jams. Or defrosted slightly, sprinkled with sugar, and served with cream.	Sugarless pack.	Sort, wash and drain well. Spread on trays. Cover and freeze. Pour frozen berries into polyethylene bags.
Sour Cherries	Pies. (Defrost slightly to prevent soggy crust.)	Dry sugar pack: 1 cup sugar to 4 cups prepared fruit.	Sort, wash, stem and pit. Pack in rigid containers, leaving 1 inch headspace.
Sweet Cherries	Pies.	Dry sugar pack: ¾ cup sugar to 4 cups prepared fruit.	Prepare as above.
Cranberries	Bread, pies and relishes.	Sugarless pack.	See blueberries. Or make cranberry sauce, cool; pack in rigid containers, leaving 1 inch headspace.

Red and Black Currants	Dry sugar pack: 1 cup sugar to 3 cups fruit.	Sort, wash, and top and tail currants. Crush a few berries to help dissolve sugar. Pack in rigid containers, leaving 1 inch headspace.
	Sugarless pack.	Prepare as above. Pack in polyethylene bags.
Gooseberries	Sugarless pack or Dry sugar pack: 1 cup sugar to 4 cups fruit.	See blueberries. See currants.
Grapefruit and Orange Fruit Cocktail	Thin syrup pack. Add ascorbic acid.	Peel and section fruit; remove pith, membrane and seeds. Pack in rigid containers. Cover with syrup, leaving 1 inch headspace.
Fruit cocktail.		See grapefruit and orange fruit cocktail. Pack in rigid containers, leaving ½-inch headspace.
Oranges	Dry sugar pack: ¾ cup sugar to 4 oranges.	
Desserts and fruit salad. To serve: Defrost slightly and combine with other fruit, or serve slightly defrosted with a drizzle of Cointreau or other liqueur.		
Peaches and Nectarines	Dry sugar pack: ⅔ cup sugar to 4 cups prepared fruit. Add ascorbic acid.	Wash and blanch 1 minute. Remove skin, halve and pit. Drop into brine bath. Pack in rigid containers, leaving 1 inch headspace.
Desserts.	Medium syrup pack. Add ascorbic acid.	Prepare as above. Pack in rigid containers. Pour syrup over, leaving 1 inch headspace.
Pears	Thin syrup pack.	Select firm crisp-textured pears. Prepare syrup. Wash, peel and core. Drop into brine bath. Heat syrup. Poach pears in syrup for 2 minutes, drain and cool. Pack in rigid containers. Cool syrup and pour over pears, leaving 1 inch headspace.

FRUIT PREPARATION CHART

Fruit	For Use In	Type of Pack	Preparation
Pineapple	Desserts.	Thin or medium syrup pack, according to tartness of fruit.	Peel, core, and remove eyes. Slice, dice, or cut into chunks. Pack in rigid containers. Cover with syrup, leaving 1 inch headspace.
	Desserts and pies.	Dry sugar pack: 1 cup sugar to 8 cups fruit.	Prepare as above. Pack in rigid containers, leaving 1 inch headspace.
Plums	Pies.	Dry sugar pack: ⅔ cup sugar to 4 cups fruit.	Wash, halve and pit. Pack in rigid containers, leaving ½-inch headspace.
	Stewed fruit and puddings.	Thin syrup pack.	Prepare fruit. Pack in rigid containers. Pour syrup over, leaving 1 inch headspace.
	Jams.	Sugarless pack.	Wash, halve and pit, or leave whole. Pack in polyethylene bags or rigid containers.
Raspberries	Jams, desserts, mousses, ice cream, and pies.	Sugarless pack.	Select firm, ripe, fresh-picked raspberries. Sort, stem and wash. Pack in rigid containers, leaving 1 inch headspace.
	Desserts and pies.	Dry sugar pack: ½ cup sugar to 4 cups raspberries.	Prepare fruit. Gently mix in sugar. Allow to stand until dissolved, about 8 to 10 minutes. Pack in rigid containers, leaving ½-inch headspace.
Rhubarb	Pies, puddings, and jams.	Sugarless pack.	Trim root and leaves. Wash and cut into 1- to 2-inch lengths. Package in polyethylene bags.
Strawberries	Pies, desserts, and jams.	Sugarless pack.	Select firm, ripe, fresh-picked berries. Wash, drain well and hull. Pack in rigid containers, leaving 1 inch headspace.
	Desserts and pies.	Dry sugar pack: ½ cup sugar to 4 cups prepared berries.	See raspberries.

FREEZING VEGETABLES

Select young, tender, fresh-picked vegetables for freezing and process them as soon as possible. Produce begins to deteriorate as soon as it is picked, and the natural sugar present in some vegetables (such as peas and corn) changes to starch. It's important to pick or purchase only as many vegetables as you can process in one day. If delay is unavoidable, spread the produce on trays and store it in the refrigerator. With the exception of cabbage, white potatoes, salad greens and whole tomatoes, most vegetables freeze well.

Blanching

After vegetables have been harvested, the enzymes responsible for the maturing, and eventual decay, of the vegetable continue to work. This enzyme action will continue in the freezer, unless steps are taken to halt it, and the vegetables will lose colour, flavour, vitamins and their firm texture. In order to stop enzyme action, most vegetables must be blanched (placed in boiling water for a few minutes) before freezing. In addition to halting enzyme action, blanching softens vegetables, making them easier to pack.

The amount of time required for proper blanching depends on the size and texture of the vegetable. Peas can be blanched in two minutes, but corn on the cob takes eleven minutes. Although most vegetables are blanched before freezing, there are some vegetables that can be prepared for freezing by other methods. Broccoli is better steamed, mushrooms can be sautéed in butter, and sweet potatoes and winter squash can be baked in the oven.

Sort, wash, trim and cut vegetables. Work with about one to one-and-a-half pounds of vegetables at a time so they can be processed quickly in an organized, streamlined manner. Use approximately eighteen cups of water to blanch one pound of vegetables. Place prepared vegetables in a basket and lower the filled basket into rapidly boiling water. Maintain high heat so the water returns to a boil as quickly as possible. Cover and start timing as soon as vegetables are in the water. Follow timing schedules on tables accurately. Underblanching can stimulate enzyme activity and overblanching can cause a loss of nutritive value, flavour and colour. Stir leafy vegetables during blanching to ensure even distribution of heat.

Prepare an ice-cold water bath for cooling vegetables, using ice cubes and cold water. When blanching is finished, plunge vegetables into a cold-water bath for the same length of time they were immersed in hot water.

Packaging and Freezing

After vegetables have been completely cooled, drain on paper towels and pack in rigid containers or moisture- and vapour proof polyethylene bags. Press as much air as possible out of bags, twist neck of bag, double over, and secure with a twist tie. Label and freeze.

Place sealed, labeled containers in the coldest part of the freezer as soon as possible after processing. Leave space for cold air to circulate around each package. After twenty-four hours put containers anywhere in the freezer.

Using Frozen Vegetables

With the exception of corn on the cob, it is not necessary to thaw vegetables before cooking. Frozen vegetables may be steamed, or cooked in a small amount of salted, boiling water. Some frozen vegetables, such as sliced summer squash, can be sautéed in butter or margarine. You can put frozen vegetables directly into a casserole or stew.

It is not necessary to cook frozen vegetables for as long as fresh vegetables. Since blanching and freezing partially soften vegetables, cooking time is reduced about 50 %.

Storage Time for Fruits and Vegetables (0°F or lower)	
Citrus fruit	3 to 4 months
Other fruit	12 months
Mushrooms	3 months
Onions	3 to 6 months
Peppers	6 months
Potatoes, French fried	3 months
Vegetables, precooked	1 month
Other vegetables (blanched)	12 months

VEGETABLE PREPARATION CHART

Vegetable	Preparation	Blanching Time	Chilling Time	Method of Packing	Cooking
Asparagus	Select young, tender stalks. Wash well to remove sand. Remove tough lower stalks and scales. Trim to uniform length to fit container. (Trimmings can be blanched and frozen separately for use in soup.) Blanch in boiling water, chill and drain.	Thin stalks 2 minutes. Medium stalks 3 minutes. Large stalks 4 minutes.	Same as blanching.	Pack in rigid containers, one tip up and one tip down. Seal and freeze. Or freeze on trays and pack in polyethylene bags.	Drop frozen into small amount of boiling salted water, cover and cook 3 to 5 minutes or until just tender.
Green or Wax Beans	Select young, tender, small, seeded beans. Sort and wash well. Trim stem and blossom ends. Leave whole, cut into 1-inch pieces, or julienne. Blanch, chill and drain.	Whole beans 3 minutes. Cut or sliced beans 2 minutes.	Same as blanching.	Pack in rigid containers, leaving ½-inch headspace. Or freeze on trays and pack in polyethylene bags.	Drop frozen into small amount of boiling salted water, cover and cook. Whole: 5 to 7 minutes. Cut or sliced: 5 to 6 minutes.
Lima Beans	Select young, tender beans. Wash pods and remove seeds. Blanch, chill and drain.	Small beans 2 minutes. Medium beans 3 minutes. Large beans 4 minutes.	Same as blanching.	Pack in rigid containers, leaving ½-inch headspace. Or freeze on trays and pack in polyethylene bags.	Drop frozen into boiling salted water. Use 1 cup of water for 2 cups of lima beans. Cover and cook 5 to 8 minutes.

Vegetable	Preparation	Blanching Time	Chilling Time	Method of Packing	Cooking
Beets	Select small beets 1½ to 3 inches in diameter. Wash well; cook in boiling water until tender. Drain, chill and peel. Package small beets whole. Slice, quarter, or dice larger beets.	Cook until tender. Small beets 25 to 30 minutes. Large beets 40 to 50 minutes.	Approximately same as cooking time.	Pack into rigid containers, leaving ½-inch headspace for cut beets. Or freeze on trays and pack in polyethylene bags.	Thaw in refrigerator 2 to 6 hours according to size of pack. Serve hot or cold.
Broccoli	Select dark green, compact heads. Trim coarse stems. Split thick stems. Wash and soak in salt water to remove insects. Blanch or steam. Chill and drain.	Small spears 3 minutes. Large spears 4 minutes. Or steam: Small spears 4 minutes. Large spears 5 minutes.	Same as blanching.	Pack into rigid containers, 1 stalk up and 1 stalk down. Or freeze on trays and pack in polyethylene bags.	Drop frozen into small amount of salted water. Cover and cook 5 to 10 minutes.
Brussels Sprouts	Select small, young sprouts. Trim ends and, if necessary, outer leaves. Wash thoroughly.	Small sprouts 3 minutes. Medium sprouts 4 minutes. Large sprouts 5 minutes.	Same as blanching.	Pack into rigid containers. Or freeze on trays and pack in polyethylene bags.	Drop frozen into small amount of boiling salted water. Cover and cook 5 to 8 minutes.

	Preparation	Blanching time	Chill	Packaging	To cook
Cabbage	Select young, firm heads. Trim off outer leaves. Cut into thin wedges or separate into leaves. Blanch, chill and drain.	Medium-size heads 1½ minutes.	Same as blanching.	Freeze on trays and pack in polyethylene bags.	Drop frozen into small amount of boiling salted water or seasoned tomato sauce. Cover and cook 5 to 6 minutes. Or use whole leaves for cabbage rolls.
Carrots	Select small, baby carrots. Wash well, scrape and trim ends. Small carrots may be left whole. Dice larger carrots or cut into rings or spears. Blanch, chill and drain.	Whole baby carrots 5 minutes. Cut carrots 3 minutes.	Same as blanching.	Pack, leaving ½-inch headspace. Or freeze whole carrots on trays and pack in polyethylene bags.	Drop frozen into small amount of boiling salted water. Cover and cook about 5 to 6 minutes, or add to stews or casseroles.
Cauliflower	Select firm, white heads. Trim outer leaves. Break into 1-inch flowerets. Soak if necessary. Blanch, chill and drain.	1-inch flowerets 3 minutes.	Same as blanching.	Pack in rigid containers. Or freeze on trays and pack in polyethylene bags.	Drop frozen in small amount of boiling salted water. Cover and cook 5 to 8 minutes.
Corn (on cob)	Select young, tender ears. Process as quickly as possible after picking. Remove husks and silk. Trim ends. Wash in cold water. Separate ears into uniform sizes. Blanch, chill and drain.	1½-inch diameter 8 minutes. 2-inch diameter 9 minutes. Larger ears 10 minutes.	Same as blanching.	Pack in rigid containers or polyethylene bags.	Thaw almost completely before cooking. Drop into boiling salted water to cover. Cook 3 to 5 minutes. (Sugar and milk can be added to water for additional flavor.)

Vegetable	Preparation	Blanching Time	Chilling Time	Method of Packing	Cooking
Cut Corn	Select young, tender ears. Blanch according to size of ears. Cool, drain and cut corn from cob.	4 to 5 minutes, according to size.	Same as blanching.	Pack in rigid containers or polyethylene bags.	Place in double boiler with a little milk, bake in the oven, or add to casseroles.
Eggplant	Select medium size firm eggplants. Wash, trim and cut into slices ¾ inches thick. Blanch in water containing 1 teaspoon citric acid to 4 cups of water to prevent discolouration.	4 minutes.	Same as blanching.	Freeze on trays and pack in rigid containers or in polyethylene bags.	Defrost partially. Dip slices in egg and bread crumbs for frying, or use in casseroles as is, or diced.
Greens, Spinach, Chard, Beet tops	Select young, tender leaves. Discard coarse stems. Wash thoroughly in cold water to remove sand. Blanch, stirring to prevent leaves from sticking together. Cool and drain.	2 minutes.	Same as blanching. Draining may not be as complete with greens as other vegetables.	Pack into rigid containers, leaving 1 inch headspace.	May be partially defrosted in order to break apart slightly. Drop into boiling salted water cover and simmer 3 to 5 minutes.
Kohlrabi	Select small, young kohlrabi. Trim off tops and roots, and peel. Leave whole or dice. Blanch, chill and drain.	Whole kohlrabi 3 minutes. Diced kohlrabi 1 minute.	Same as blanching.	Package in rigid containers or polyethylene bags.	Drop frozen into small amount of boiling salted water. Cover and cook 8 to 12 minutes.

Mushrooms	Select fresh mushrooms. Wipe to remove soil. Trim ends. Sort into large and small sizes. Slice large mushrooms, leave small mushrooms whole. Sauté in butter until almost cooked. Chill. Spread undrained mushrooms on a plate and chill in refrigerator.	Sauté until almost cooled.	Chill in refrigerator or freezer until cold.	Pack in rigid containers, leaving ½-inch headspace.	Heat in saucepan or skillet. Or defrost slightly to separate, chop, and add to casseroles or other dishes.
Okra	Select young, tender seed pods. Sort into small and large sizes. Trim stems and wash well. Blanch and chill.	4 inch pods 3 minutes. Larger pods 5 minutes.	Same as blanching.	Pack in rigid containers. Or freeze on trays and pack in polyethylene bags.	Add to soup or stews.
Onions	Peel and cut into ½-inch slices. Blanch and chill. Peel and leave whole. Blanch and chill.	2 minutes. 3 to 7 minutes, heated through.	Same as blanching.	Pack in rigid containers or in double polyethylene bags to prevent transfer of flavours.	Use in soup, stews or casseroles.
Peas	Select young, sweet peas. Freeze promptly after harvesting. Shell, blanch and chill.	1½ minutes.	Same as blanching.	Pack in rigid containers, leaving 1 inch headspace. Or pack in polyethylene bags.	Drop frozen into small amount of boiling salted water 5 to 7 minutes.
Green or Sweet Red Bell Peppers	Wash well. Remove stems, seeds and membranes. Leave whole. Or cut in half, remove seeds and membranes.	No blanching. No blanching.		Pack in polyethylene bags. As above.	Defrost slightly before stuffing and baking. Dice or cut into strips. Use in soup, stews and casseroles.

Vegetable	Preparation	Blanching Time	Chilling Time	Method of Packing	Cooking
Potatoes for French Frying	Select mature potatoes. Wash, peel and cut into ½-inch sticks. Blanch, chill and drain.	2 minutes. Or dry fry in 375°F cooking oil.	Same as blanching.	Drain. Freeze on trays and pack in polyethylene bags.	Defrost. Deep fry in 375°F cooking oil.
Pumpkin and Winter Squash	Cook until tender in oven, boiling water or steam. Scrape pulp from rind. Mash or sieve. Cool immediately in refrigerator.	Cook until tender.	Refrigerate until cool.	Pack into rigid containers, leaving ½-inch headspace.	Defrost pumpkin and use in pies, bread, or cakes. Heat winter squash in double boiler.
Summer Squash	Select young, uniform size squash. Wash, trim ends, and cut in ½-inch slices. Blanch, chill and drain.	3 minutes.	Same as blanching.	Pack into rigid containers, leaving ½-inch headspace. Or freeze on trays and pack in poly-ethylene bags.	Drop frozen into small amount of boiling, salted water. Cover and cook 2 to 3 minutes. Or defrost slightly and sauté in butter.
Tomatoes	Select firm, ripe tomatoes. Wash, blanch to loosen skin, peel, core and quarter. Simmer in covered saucepan 10 to 15 minutes. Purée, if desired. Simmer slowly to make concentrate. Cool.	1 minute for easy skin removal.	Cool tomatoes in pan set on iced water.	Pack into rigid containers leaving 1 inch headspace.	Can be frozen in ice cube trays for use as flavouring in soup, sauces, and gravies.
Turnips	Select young roots. Wash, trim ends and peel. Dice, blanch, cool and drain. Prepare in the same way as carrots, or mash and season.	3 minutes.	Same as blanching.	Pack in rigid containers, leaving ½-inch headspace.	Drop frozen into small amount of boiling water. Cover and cook 8 to 12 minutes.

10 DRYING FOOD

The process of drying to preserve food goes all the way back to the Stone Age. It was the natural environment that provided the first method of preserving food, probably quite by accident. Ancient men (or was it women?) discovered that when certain foods were placed in the sun for long periods of time, they became hard and dry and, in this state, did not decompose.

Today the drying of food is still considered one of the simplest methods of food preservation. In addition to their growing interest in canning and freezing, many people have begun to experiment with food drying and have found it to be a simple and satisfactory process.

Drying removes most of the water content from food, and much of the bulk. The space required to store dried food is therefore minimal and sophisticated storage methods are not needed. All you need are clean, airtight containers and a cool, dark place for storage.

HOW DRYING PRESERVES FOOD

The object of all methods of food preservation is the creation of an environment that will allow food to be stored safely for extended periods of time. Simultaneously, the environment must be unfavourable to food spoilage organisms so the food will not be attacked by these organisms during storage. When food is canned, it is placed in sealed jars and heat is applied to destroy or inactivate spoilage agents. The airtight containers prevent recontamination of

145

the food. When food is frozen, the low temperature at which food is stored inhibits the growth or activity of spoilage organisms.

The principle of food preservation by drying is that microorganisms require a certain amount of moisture in order to grow. If enough water is removed from food, these organisms cannot grow, and food spoilage is prevented.

DRYING METHODS

There are three methods by which food can be dried successfully: sun drying, oven drying, and in scientifically designed food dryers. Food should not be dried over the vents of a furnace. Occasionally a furnace emits particles of combustion that, while generally unnoticeable in the air, are absorbed by food, and may be harmful if eaten.

Sun Drying

Fruits such as grapes, prunes, apricots, dates and figs can be dried in the sun if you live in an area that has constant, hot, dry heat and very little humidity. There are only a few areas in North America where food can be dried outdoors successfully. These areas include the central region of California and the southwestern states. In Canada and he United States the plains east of the Rockies also have long periods of dry, hot weather. But outdoor drying is difficult because food may be contaminated by dust, polluted air, insects, or animals.

Spread prepared produce on trays (see Equipment) and cover with cheesecloth. Place trays in direct sun on supports that will permit air to circulate freely around trays. Periodically stir food and turn pieces of food over. Bring food inside at night. Testing for dryness can begin after two days.

Oven Drying

Although it is possible to dry food in an oven, it's tricky because it is necessary to maintain a constant low oven temperature between 120°F and 150°F, the exact temperature determined by the kind of food being dried. You will need an oven thermometer to determine if your oven can maintain the constant low temperature that is required. The wide variation of temperature that an oven usually generates if the thermostat goes off and on to maintain a specific temperature can be detrimental to the food being dried. The oven door of a gas oven must be left open about six inches to allow moisture to escape. The door of an electric oven should be left open one inch. Don't attempt to dry more than one or two trays of food at a time because, as humidity builds up in the oven, the process of drying is lengthened. Be sure that broiler does not go on at any time during processing.

Food Dryers

The most satisfactory method of drying food is with an electric dryer that provides a controlled environment of warm, circulating air which removes moisture from the food. Some features to look for when purchasing a dryer are:

An adjustable thermostat offering a wide range of temperatures for drying a variety of food products.

Trays that are easily cleaned and highly porous, made from a food-safe material. Typical screen-type designs are desirable for maximum air circulation.

Controlled air flow design that provides circulation of warm air throughout the dryer. Temperature should be constant at all points in the dryer so that trays will not have to be rotated.

Safety features such as U.L. approved parts.

EQUIPMENT

With the exception of a special electric food dryer, most of the equipment required to dry food is available in a reasonably well equipped kitchen.

Trays: Select (or make) wooden trays that are slatted, woven, or perforated so that warm air can circulate around food. Don't use solid wood or galvanized metal trays. Trays should be made of a material that will not be affected by heat, will not discolour food, and will not flavour food in any way. Pine, oak, redwood and wood that is still green should not be used.

Basket: Use when blanching or steaming fruit and vegetables.

Scales: Use scales to weigh food before and after drying in order to determine if enough water has been removed.

Airtight containers: Glass jars, plastic containers, polyethylene bags and ties for storage of food.

PREPARATION OF PRODUCE

Produce to be dried should be flawless and in peak condition. Food should be prepared under sanitary conditions and must be washed and drained before preparation. Don't prepare more food for drying than you can process promptly and easily.

Ascorbic Acid to Prevent Discolouration

Special treatment must be given to fruit that darkens when exposed to air. When these fruits are canned or frozen they are placed in a brine bath or a solution of ascorbic acid to prevent browning. When food is dried, the prepared cut food is exposed to air for several hours during the drying process and therefore is particularly susceptible to discolouration. Ascorbic acid (vitamin C) does an excellent job of preventing undesirable colour changes in fruit. But more ascorbic acid is needed in drying food than in canning or freezing, and different strengths of ascorbic acid solution must be used for different fruits. Make a solution of 2½ teaspoons of ascorbic acid to 1 cup of water for fruit that

148

darkens easily; 1 teaspoon of ascorbic acid to 1 cup of water for other fruit (or follow package instructions). One cup of ascorbic acid solution is enough for five cups of cut fruit. Dip prepared fruit in the solution, coating all cut surfaces, or sprinkle it over the fruit. Don't soak fruit because it will absorb water and lengthen the drying process.

Hot Water Dip

Some fruits (grapes, cherries, blueberries and plums) have a heavy skin with a wax-like finish that retards evaporation. To help speed the drying process, these fruits must be given special treatment. Bring water to a boil in a saucepan and reduce heat so water simmers. Wash fruit and place it in a basket. Immerse the filled basket in hot water for the time recommended on tables. Remove from hot water and plunge immediately into ice-cold water. Keep fruit in cold water until cool, then drain on paper toweling. Proceed with next step for drying, following instructions on tables.

Steaming

Steaming is essential for vegetables to be dried because it retards the action of enzymes. It is also recommended for some fruit because it inhibits discolouration, protects some nutrients, and softens and loosens fruit skins so that the process of drying is speeded.

Fill a saucepan with two to three inches of water and bring to a boil over high heat. Place prepared cut fruit or vegetables in a steamer or basket. Don't overcrowd basket because steam must reach all food equally. Place basket over (not in) boiling water. Cover with tight-fitting lid, reduce heat and simmer for time recommended on tables. Remove food and place in a single layer on paper toweling. Cover with toweling to absorb excess moisture.

DRYING FRUIT

Select ripe, flawless fruit. Wash in cold water and drain well. Treat as necessary with ascorbic acid solution, hot water dip or steam. Process according to tables until tests indicate food is dry. Pasteurize, cool, package, label and store.

FRUIT PREPARATION CHART

Fruit	Preparation	Prevention of Discolouration	Steaming Time	Drying Times and Temperatures For Home Food Dryer	Characteristics Of Dried Product
Apples	Wash, peel and core. Cut into ⅛-inch slices. Treat for discolouration as each apple is prepared.	Coat each slice with ascorbic acid solution.	5 minutes.	6 to 7 hours. 130°F for 1 hour. 150°F until almost dry. 140° for final drying. Test for dryness. Pasteurize 15 minutes.	Leathery, no moisture when squeezed.
Apricots and Nectarines	Select ripe apricots. Wash, halve and pit. Treat for discolouration.	Coat cut surfaces with ascorbic acid solution.	15 minutes.	12 to 14 hours for halves. Drying temperatures: See apples.	Leathery, rubbery, no moisture when squeezed.
Hard-skinned berries (cranberries, blueberries, black currants, etc.)	Wash and trim stems and blossom ends if necessary. Dip in boiling water 15 to 30 seconds. Plunge into cold water. Drain on paper towels.	Not necessary.	None.	4 to 5 hours. 130°F for 1 hour. 140°F for remaining time. Test for dryness. Pasteurize 15 minutes.	Hard, no moisture. Berries rattle on trays.
Cherries	Wash, halve and pit.	Not necessary.	None.	5 to 6 hours. 120°F for 1 hour. 140°F until almost dry. 135°F for final drying. Test for dryness. Pasteurize 15 minutes.	Leathery, sticky.

	Preparation	Pretreatment	Blanching/Steaming	Drying	Test for dryness
Figs	Cut large figs in half; leave small figs whole. Whole figs: Dip in boiling water 30 to 40 seconds. Plunge into cold water. Drain on paper towels. Halved figs: Steam.	Not necessary.	20 minutes.	4 to 6 hours. 120°F for 1 hour. 145°F until almost dry. 130°F for final drying. Test for dryness. Pasteurize 15 minutes.	Leathery, slightly sticky, soft.
Grapes	Select seedless variety. Wash and remove stems. Dip in boiling water 15 to 30 seconds. Plunge into cold water.	Not necessary.	None.	Drying temperatures: See cherries.	Fairly pliable flesh, slightly sticky.
Peaches	Select freestone variety. Blanch 60 seconds in boiling water to loosen skins. Cool quickly. Peel, halve, pit and slice. Treat for discolouration as each peach is prepared.	Coat peaches with ascorbic acid solution.	Halves: 15 to 20 minutes. Slices: 8 minutes.	6 to 7 hours. 130°F for 1 hour. 155°F until almost dry. 140°F for final drying. Test for dryness. Pasteurize 15 minutes.	Leathery, tough.
Pears	Allow pears to ripen. Wash, peel and core. Remove fibrous vein. Halve or slice and treat for discolouration as each fruit is prepared.	Coat each slice with ascorbic acid solution.	Halves: 20 minutes. Slices: 5 minutes.	5 to 7 hours. 130°F for 1 hour. 150°F until almost dry. 140°F for final drying. Test for dryness. Pasteurize 15 minutes.	Leathery, no moisture when cut or squeezed.
Plums	Wash plums. Leave whole. Dip in boiling water 30 to 45 seconds. Plunge into cold water. Drain on paper towels.	Not necessary.	Whole: 15 minutes. Sliced: 5 minutes.	Whole: 14 hours. Halves: 8 hours. Sliced: 6 hours. 120°F for 1 hour. 150°F until almost dry. 140°F for final drying. Test for dryness.	Pliable and leathery.

DRYING VEGETABLES

Select young, tender, flawless vegetables.
Wash in cold water and drain well.
Prepare vegetables as indicated in tables.
Steam for recommended length of time.
Dry process according to tables until tests indicate food is dry.
Pasteurize, cool, package, label and store.

TESTING FOR DRYNESS

Don't attempt to compare produce dried at home with commercially dried food. Commercial processors use highly sophisticated industrial equipment and preservatives and, as a result, commercially dried food has a higher moisture content than food dried at home. The preservatives used protect dried food from the spoilage that can occur with the higher moisture content.

Remove one or two pieces of processed food from the dryer and allow them to cool before testing for dryness. Warm food will seem softer and more moist than food that has cooled.

To test fruit, cut a piece of cooled, processed fruit and squeeze it. There should be no moisture apparent and the fruit should feel "rubbery" or "leathery."

To test vegetables, shake the drying tray. Vegetables usually rattle when they are dry. They will feel tough and brittle.

Food can also be tested for dryness by weight. Weigh food before drying and then weigh it again near the end of the drying process. When the weight has dropped fifty percent the food is approximately two-thirds dry.

PASTEURIZATION

After drying has been completed, it is recommended that a final heat treatment be given in order to pasteurize food before storage. This treatment is necessary to destroy harmful bacteria.

Spread dried fruit or vegetables on trays (don't crowd), and place the trays in a preheated 175°F oven. Heat vegetables ten minutes and fruit, which is usually cut into larger pieces, fifteen minutes. Remove food from oven, cover loosely with clean cloth, cool and package.

PACKAGING DRIED FOOD

Dried food should be stored in well-filled, tightly covered containers or in polyethylene bags. There should be as little air as possible in containers because air that comes in contact with food during storage causes changes in the food. Dried food is like blotting paper; it absorbs any moisture that comes its way. As a result, food is likely to spoil during storage if containers are not airtight.

Food must be completely cool before it can be packaged. Moisture may build up in the container if food is packaged while still warm. Containers should be clean and thoroughly dry. If you notice any moisture on the inside of a container, remove the food immediately and return it to the drying oven.

Be sure containers are sweet smelling and that no odours remain from food previously stored in the container. Close containers securely, label and store in a cool, dark, dry place, away from possible contamination by insects or animals.

COOKING DRIED FRUIT

Fruit to be served stewed or as a compote should be covered with water and allowed to stand for several hours. After fruit has soaked, place it in a saucepan with the water, cover and simmer ten to fifteen minutes, adding more water if necessary. Sweeten to taste just before serving. Don't sweeten prior to cooking because sugar added during cooking may toughen fruit.

Fruit to be used in pies or other cooked dishes should be placed in just enough water to cover and allowed to sit until water has been absorbed. Don't add an excessive amount of water, because water not absorbed by the fruit will contain valuable nutrients that may be lost if the fruit is drained. Add more water only if fruit is tough. Once the water has been absorbed the fruit will be plump and ready for use in a recipe.

COOKING DRIED VEGETABLES

Cover vegetables with cold water and allow them to soak several hours until vegetables resemble fresh produce. Don't add more water to vegetables than they can absorb. After vegetables have soaked, place them in a saucepan with a small amount of water, cover and simmer until tender. Add more water if necessary. Season to taste and serve. Once vegetables have been soaked it is also possible to add them to casseroles, soup, and stews.

Vegetables that have been precooked prior to drying should be soaked in water until restored to original appearance and texture. Heat in a small amount of water, steam or sauté in butter or margarine. Season to taste and serve.

DRYING HERBS

Herbs can be dried easily. Pick herbs just before they flower. Cut them early in the day when they are dry, but not yet warmed by the sun. Pull off dead leaves, hold by the stem, and rinse in cold running water to wash off dust, soil and dirt. Shake dry and place between paper towels to absorb moisture.

When herbs are completely dry, place them in a large brown paper bag. Close the end of the bag tightly and hang the bag in a warm, dry place. Don't hang it in a very hot area or directly in the sun.

When completely dry, remove herbs from bag, pull off leaves, and crumble them. Place crushed leaves in dry, air tight jars. Label and store in a cool, dry, dark place.

VEGETABLE PREPARATION CHART

Vegetable	Preparation	Steaming Time	Drying Temperatures	Characteristics of Dried Product
Green and Yellow Snap Beans	Wash and trim stems and flower ends. Leave whole.	Small: 15 minutes. Large: 20 minutes.	120°F for 1 hour. 150°F until almost dry. 130°F for final drying. Test for dryness. Pasteurize 10 minutes.	Hard and brittle.
Lima Beans	Shell.	10 minutes.	140°F for 1 hour. 160°F until nearly dry. 130°F for final drying. Test for dryness. Pasteurize 10 minutes.	Hard and brittle.
Beets	Use only small beets. Trim stalks, leaving 1 to 2 inches of stalk to prevent bleeding. Cover with boiling water and simmer until tender (about 30 minutes). Peel and trim ends. Cut into ⅛-inch slices.	30-45 minutes.	120°F for 1 hour. 150°F until nearly dry. 130°F for final drying. Test for dryness. Pasteurize 10 minutes.	Tough but flexible.
Carrots	Use young, tender carrots. Wash well or scrape.	20 to 30 minutes, or until just tender. Trim stem and root ends. Cut into ⅛-inch slices.	See beets.	Tough but flexible.
Celery	Wash stalks. Cut into ¼-inch pieces. Cut large pieces in half.	4 minutes.	130°F for 1 hour. 150°F until almost dry. 130°F for final drying. Test for dryness. Pasteurize 10 minutes.	Brittle.

VEGETABLE PREPARATION CHART

Vegetable	Preparation	Steaming Time	Drying Temperatures	Characteristics of Dried Product
Mushrooms	Select fresh, tightly closed mushrooms. Wipe with damp cloth. Cut stems into ⅛-inch pieces; slice caps into ⅛-inch pieces.	12 to 15 minutes.	130°F for 1 hour. 150°F until nearly dry. 140°F for final drying. Test for dryness. Pasteurize 10 minutes. (Dry caps and stems separately.)	Brittle.
Onions	Peel and slice into ⅛-inch rings.	None.	140°F until almost dry. Onions scorch easily, so watch carefully. Reduce heat to 130°F for final drying period. Test for dryness.	Crisp.
Peas	See lima beans.			
Hot Peppers	Wash well. Thread on a string, leaving a space between each pepper. Hang in warm dry place, indoors or outdoors. Dried pepper will shrink and be dark-coloured and crisp.			

INDEX